JE MOURRAI MOINS BÊTE:

200 French expressions to help you die less stupid

Bonne lecture!
Clare Jones

Written by Clare Jones

Illustrated by Tamsin Edwards

Copyright © 2015 Clare Jones

2nd edition 2020

All rights reserved.

ISBN-10:1519107684

ISBN-13:978-1519107688

Printed by CreateSpace, An Amazon.com Company

CONTENTS

Preface 6

Introduction 7

1   *Les connaissances* – knowledge 9

   Être ingénieux et profiter au maximum – being resourceful and making the most of things 21

   La diplomatie et la prise de décision – diplomacy and decision making 25

   Quiz 1 30

   Answers 1 35

2   *Les premiers pas* – first steps or going for it 36

   Perdre du temps et travailler sans se fatiguer – wasting time and taking it easy at work 45

   Quiz 2 54

   Answers 2 59

3   *Travailler dur* – working hard 60

   Quiz 3 80

   Answers 3 84

4   *Les problèmes* – problems 84

   Identifier ses priorités – prioritizing 102

   Quiz 4 105

   Answers 4 110

5	*Les professions et les carrières* – professions and careers 111	
	Aller bien – going well 116	
	Quiz 5 127	
	Answers 5 132	
6	*L'aide et les dettes* – help and indebtedness 133	
	Le travail facile – easy work 144	
	Quiz 6 152	
	Answers 6 157	
7	*Les heures de travail et les habitudes* – working hours and habits 158	
	Avoir de l'influence ou du pouvoir – having influence or power 162	
	Une sale affaire – nasty business 166	
	Quiz 7 178	
	Answers 7 183	
8	*Avoir du mal* – struggling 184	
	Céder – giving in 191	
	L'échec – failure 193	
	Quiz 8 206	
	Answers 8 211	
9	*Discipliner et renvoyer* – disciplining and sacking	

212

Les manières rudes – rough manner 222

Faire des affaires ensemble – doing business together 227

Quiz 9 232

Answers 9 237

10   *Voir clair et évaluer les problèmes* – seeing clearly and getting perspective 238

Résoudre des problèmes et surmonter des difficultés – resolving problems and overcoming difficulties 248

Les bosseurs infatigables– tireless workers 252

Quiz 10 258

Answers 10 262

Afterword 263

Complete list of expressions 264

More about the author 281

More about the illustrator 282

By the same author and illustrator 283

Bibliography 284

Websites 285

Index 288

Preface

Why did I write this book? Because French expressions fascinate me and there is simply not enough time in my lessons to share all the knowledge I have discovered. I couldn't find another book written in English which not only gives literal translations of French idioms and examples of their usage but also explains the origins and the cultural significance of them, so I decided to write the book myself. I am sure you will find my enthusiasm contagious!

I acknowledge the endless patience of my French pen friend and teaching colleague, Florence Pierrard. She has overseen the writing of this book and has made sure that the French I have used sounds natural to native ears. Many thanks also go to Christian Voleau, Michel Meslin, Catherine Pettet and Jennifer Pettet.

Introduction

Because the French language is rich in figurative expressions, I had to decide upon an area to focus my attentions and I chose the world of work. The themes of success and failure, struggling, facing difficulties and resolving problems are all common to our everyday experiences. You might be a sports enthusiast who wants to encourage others to keep trying and not to give up. You might want to complain about a builder who is lazy, or thank someone who has helped you and tell them you "owe them one". You will want to understand when your French neighbours are telling you how hard they work or how they are taking it easy now they have retired. We all need the language of business, whether we are negotiating a multimillion-pound deal or trying to get a bargain from a market stallholder. This book is aimed at anyone who wants to understand the French and the French language better, whether they work in an office in Paris or not. Throughout this text I have assumed that my readers already have a fairly good grasp of the French language and know basic pronunciation.

In choosing these particular two hundred expressions, I have tried to select those which are current and well-known. I asked the opinion of many native French speakers and was guided by their answers. The challenge has been that not every French person knows every French expression – ask an English-speaking teenager if they have heard of a list of English idioms and it's quite possible they won't know a large number of them. I have chosen expressions I have heard commonly in spoken conversations with French adults; they appear in films and television programmes or have been read in contemporary novels, newspapers and websites or in personal correspondence with my French pen friends. I apologize in advance if you try using one of these expressions and it is not recognized or understood. It is always a good idea to have another way of saying the same thing up your sleeve!

It is important to know which expressions are appropriate in which situations – you don't want to shock your new friends or colleagues by using a vulgar term when you were aiming for politeness! For that reason, I have used asterisks to show levels of informality or vulgarity.

No asterisk = safe to use in any situation

* = colloquial but acceptable in polite circles

** = very colloquial, use with care

Three asterisks would be considered very vulgar. Though I make some mention of swearwords, I have chosen not to include the more vulgar expressions here because they often sound very odd coming out of the mouths of foreigners.

I hope you share my curiosity and enjoy delving into the origin of some of the expressions. The artist, Tamsin Edwards, has illustrated the literal meaning of over 150 expressions to help you to memorize them.

Don't miss out the quiz sections. They might be a bit of a challenge but be brave! You can always use a dictionary to look up any new words you meet there. If you do well on the tests, you know you are making progress.

Amuse-toi bien!

Clare

CHAPTER 1

Les connaissances – knowledge

- *apprendre* ou *connaître les ficelles du métier** – to learn *or* to know the ropes*

Literally: to learn *or* to know the strings of the job

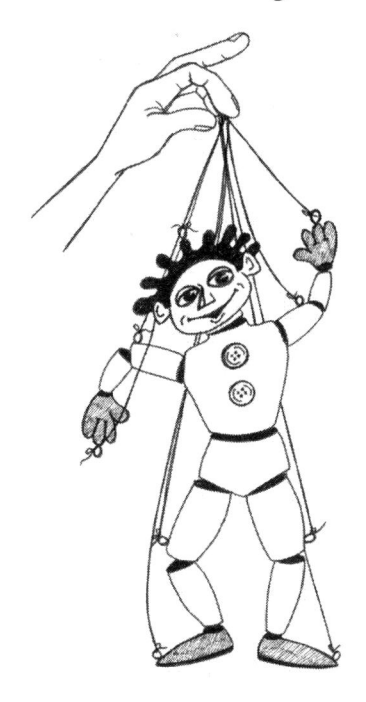

Il a passé sa jeunesse dans l'usine de son père, ce qui lui a permis d'apprendre les ficelles du métier d'industriel.

He spent his youth in his father's factory, which allowed him to learn the ropes of the manufacturing industry.

Whereas the English expression "to know the ropes" seems to have a nautical origin, to do with knowing the ropes on a ship, the French expression is not *connaître les cordes*, 'the ropes', but *connaître les ficelles*, 'the strings'. Georges Planelles does not mention boats in his discussion of the subject on his excellent website, Expressio. He suggests that the origin might have been to do with the strings of a puppet and knowing which ones to pull. He explains that, in the olden days, the word *ficelle* was linked to deception: *faire de la ficelle à quelqu'un* meant 'to deceive somebody'; *une vieille ficelle* was 'a crafty old devil' and *tirer les ficelles* ('to pull the strings') is 'to manipulate'.

According to Expressio, ***connaître les ficelles du métier*** used to have a negative meaning, such as 'to know the crude tricks of a trade', but these days it is no longer an expression of disapproval and just means 'to know the basics of a job'.

- ***apprendre sur le tas*** – to learn on the job *or* as one goes along

Literally: to learn on the pile

J'ai dû apprendre mon métier sur le tas. Je n'ai pas fait d'études ni de formation particulière.

I had to learn my trade on the job. I didn't study or do any particular training.

Why "to learn on the pile"? The word *tas* had the meaning in the 17th century of 'a building under construction' or 'stones that one cuts in the place where they will be used'. It follows that you could learn your job *sur le tas* or "in the place where you are working".

- *avoir plus d'une corde à son arc* – to have more than one string to one's bow; to have more than one means of reaching one's goal; to be capable of doing several things

Literally: to have several strings to one's bow

Je peux vous faire les traductions en anglais et aussi en allemand. Eh oui, j'ai plus d'une corde à mon arc !

I can do you the translations into English and into German too. Ah yes, I have more than one string to my bow!

We are not talking about having more than one string attached to a bow at the same time because that really wouldn't help you to hit your target. However, as Planelles points out, the clever archer would have at least one other string ready in case the first one snapped, so if his first attempt failed, he could try again with a new one. He could try in more than one way to attain his goal.

This expression dates from the 13th century, where it started out as *avoir deux cordes à son arc*. In the 17th century it became our modern version, *avoir plus d'une corde à son arc* or *avoir plusieurs cordes à son arc*.

- *connaître ou savoir sur le bout du doigt ou des doigts* – to know off pat* *or* backwards *or* inside out

Literally: to know on the tip of the finger *or* the fingers

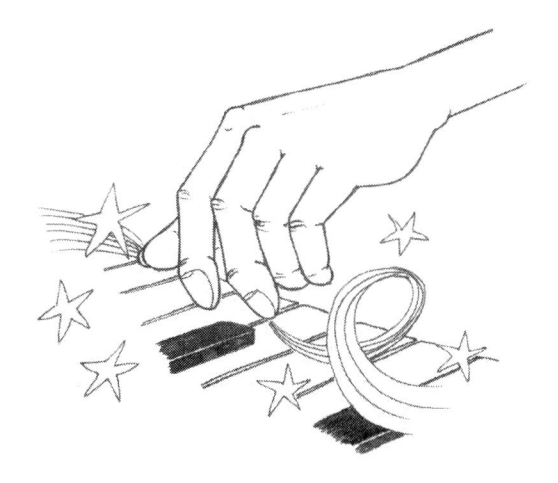

Demandez à Mme Roussel. Elle connaît la question sur le bout des doigts.

Ask Mrs Roussel. She knows the subject inside out.

It seems that the origin of this expression is disputed, so failing consensus from the experts, let's go with the most likely explanation. If someone knows a subject really well and they sit down to write about it, the knowledge seems to come pouring out from the tips of the fingers almost without effort. And if a master carpenter picks up a piece of wood to turn, his fingers are so used to performing the necessary actions, that it seems that all his knowledge and experience is concentrated in the tips of his fingers.

There is a very good French film, a psychological thriller, called *"Sur le bout des doigts"*, which was made in 2001. It is about the relationship between a jealous mother and her daughter, a child prodigy, who is an excellent pianist.

- *éclairer la lanterne de quelqu'un* – to enlighten somebody

Literally: to light somebody's lantern

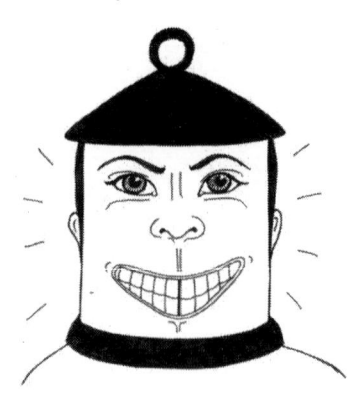

Je ne comprends pas ces accusations. Est-ce que quelqu'un peut éclairer ma lanterne ?

I don't understand these accusations. Can someone enlighten me?

This expression comes from a fable by Jean-Pierre Clarisse de Florian (1755-1794) called *"Le singe qui montre la lanterne magique"*. It tells the story of a monkey whose master travelled the fairs with a magic lantern to entertain the public. The magic lantern was a device popular in the 17th century which shone light through painted glass and projected enlarged images onto a screen to the great delight of the audience.

One day the monkey decided to put on a show for his animal friends, only he forgot to actually light the lantern, so they saw nothing of the marvels he was describing to them. Of course, his audience needed the lantern to be lit to understand the show.

When you understand nothing of what is going on around you, you might well say you are "in the dark" but if someone comes along and gives you the missing information you need to make sense of things, then you might say they have "lit your mental lantern" or "enlightened" you, enabling you to see everything clearly.

- *être à même de faire quelque chose* – to be able *or* to be in a position to do something

Literally: to be equal to doing something

Je suis la seule personne à même de comprendre ce qu'il dit, tellement son accent est fort.

I'm the only person able to understand what he's saying, his accent is so thick.

- *être au courant de quelque chose* – to know about something

Literally: to be in the current of something

Par les fonctions qu'elle a occupées, elle est au courant de beaucoup de choses qui pourraient nous être utiles.

Through the posts she has occupied, she knows about lots of things which could be of use to us.

- *être dans la course* ; ne plus être dans la course** – to be in the picture*; to be out of touch

Literally: to be in the race; to be no longer in the race

Elle n'est plus dans la course depuis longtemps, mais elle ne le voit pas.

She's been out of touch for a long time, but she doesn't see it.

(i)

Etre dans la course and **ne plus être dans la course** are also used in the sense of 'to be in the running' *or* 'to be out of the running' in the context of a candidate in an election.

- *être dans le coup* – to be in on it*; to know all about it; to know what's what

Literally: to be in the blow

Demandez à Adèle ce que signifient tous ces acronymes. Elle est dans le coup.

Ask Adèle what all these acronyms mean. She knows what's what.

(i)

Etre dans le coup can also mean 'to be with it*' or 'to be hip*'. François Ozon made a terrific film in 2002 called *"8 Femmes"*, set in the 1950s or early 60s and starring, amongst others, Catherine Deneuve, Isabelle Huppert and Emmanuelle Béart. In it, the man of the house is found with a knife in his back and a murder mystery develops where all eight women are suspects.

Each of the characters bursts into song at some point or other in the movie. One of the daughters, Catharine, played by Ludivine Sagnier, sings *"Papa t'es pas dans l'coup"* accompanied by a great dance routine. The song was originally released by the singer Sheila in 1963.

- *je me coucherai moins bête ce soir ; je mourrai moins bête* – you learn something new every day; you live and learn

Literally: I will go to bed less stupid tonight; I will die less stupid

« *Saviez-vous qu'au début du XXᵉ siècle, tous les jours à midi pile, on tirait le canon depuis la tour Eiffel ?*

– Eh ben, je mourrai moins bête ! »

"Did you know that at the beginning of the 20th century, a cannon was fired from the Eiffel Tower at exactly midday?"

"Well, you learn something new every day!"

There's a great French website and Facebook page called "*Se Coucher Moins Bête*" which is full of interesting facts. Take a look! *Tu te coucheras moins bête !*

- *savoir, c'est pouvoir (proverbe)* – knowledge is power (proverb)

Literally: knowledge is power *or* to know is to be able

La recette exacte de notre bière ne doit pas tomber entre les mains de nos concurrents. Savoir, c'est pouvoir !

The exact recipe for our beer must not fall into the hands of our competitors. Knowledge is power!

This proverb is usually attributed to the English philosopher and scientist, Francis Bacon (1561-1626). It was he who created the scientific method, the idea that all hypotheses and theories must be tested against observations of the natural world, rather than resting solely on reasoning, intuition or revelation. However, neither the English version nor the French version is a direct quotation from his writing but an approximate translation from something he wrote in Latin, and in fact, the cliché of knowledge being power goes back much further than Bacon into antiquity.

- ***si c'est toujours dans tes cordes*** – if you are still up to it; if it's still in your line

Literally: if it is still in your chords

J'ai une faveur à te demander, une petite enquête, si c'est toujours dans tes cordes.

I have a favour to ask of you, a small enquiry, if it's still in your line.

Notice that the French word *corde* is translated here literally as 'chord' rather than 'rope' or 'string' because the origin of this expression has more to do with the vocal chords than with ropes. In the 19th century *corde* meant 'the sound produced by the vocal chords' and if you said, "*ce n'est pas dans mes cordes*" you meant that something was not within your singing range.

The meaning then expanded to other areas and is now used to mean 'I'm not up to it' or 'it's not in my line'.

Être ingénieux et profiter au maximum - being resourceful and making the most of things

- *faire feu de tout bois* – to use any means available

Literally: to make fire of any wood

Ils font feu de tout bois pour produire les millions de smartphones dont ils ont besoin. Ils viennent d'ouvrir une usine en Chine.

They are using any means available to produce the millions of smartphones needed. They have just opened a factory in China.

If you are really cold, you'll burn anything you can or you'll use any means available to keep warm. There is another expression which is used less often, *faire flèche de tout bois*, 'to make arrow from any wood', which has the same meaning. This expression goes right back to the 17th century. Planelles suggests that a hungry hunter, who ran out of arrows before catching his dinner, might well have grabbed any nearly-straight branch and hacked off a few leaves to make what he needed.

- *manger à tous les râteliers* – to cash in* on all sides; to run with the hare and hunt with the hounds; to take personal benefit from all possible situations without scruples

Literally: to eat at all the racks

Toutes les techniques sont bonnes pour faire du profit – ils mangent à tous les râteliers.

They'll try any method to gain some benefit – they are cashing in on all sides.

Did you know that *un râtelier* is a set of false teeth in colloquial French? Not that that has anything to do with the *râtelier* in this expression. *Le râtelier* is also the rack that horses feed from. One greedy horse, seeing food available in its neighbour's rack, might well push his nose into that rack, as well as eating from his own. And what about humans? Well, if a person is determined to make money wherever he can, he might well try to tap every possible source of income, even if his actions might be seen by others to be unscrupulous.

The expression was used in *Les Trois Mousquetaires* by Alexandre Dumas in 1849 (you can download the whole book for free from Project Gutenberg):

« *Mon cher, soyez mousquetaire ou abbé, soyez l'un ou l'autre, mais pas l'un et l'autre, reprit Porthos. Tenez, Athos vous l'a dit encore l'autre jour : vous mangez à tous les râteliers.* »

"My dear, be a musketeer or an abbot, be one or the other, but not both," continued Porthos. "Look, Athos told you again the other day: you are cashing in on both sides."

- *se débrouiller* ou *faire avec les moyens du bord* – to cope as best as one can with what's available; to make do and mend

Literally: to cope *or* to do with the means of the edge

Pour limiter les frais de lancement, j'ai essayé de me débrouiller avec les moyens du bord.

To limit the start-up costs, I tried to make do with what I had available.

- *système D* – resourcefulness

Literally: D system

« *Comment allez-vous vous débrouiller ?*

– *Système D. Je vais vendre les objets d'art de mes parents sur leboncoin.* »

"How are you going to manage?"

"Resourcefulness. I'm going to sell my parents' antiques on leboncoin (auction website)."

The D in *système D* stands for *débrouille* or *débrouillardise*. The verb *se débrouiller* means 'to manage' or 'to cope'. *Système D* is often used to describe the culture of a whole group of people, perhaps in developing countries, who get by in very difficult circumstances through sheer resourcefulness, living day to day with whatever is to hand.

- *tirer le meilleur parti de quelque chose* – to make the most *or* the best of something

Literally: to pull the best part from something

Il fallait tirer le meilleur parti possible d'une mauvaise situation.

We had to make the best of a bad situation.

Note that we are dealing with the masculine noun here, *le parti*. *Le parti* is the word used for a political party, an option or a course of action, or is used in expressions to do with taking advantage. *La partie*, on the other hand, is the word for a part or an amount (amongst other uses). It is worth exploring a good dictionary to see the differences.

La diplomatie et la prise de décision – diplomacy and decision making

- *choisir entre la peste et le choléra* – to have to choose one of two bad options; to be between a rock and a hard place; to choose between the devil and the deep blue sea

Literally: to choose between the plague and cholera

Puisque ni l'une ni l'autre des solutions ne me convient réellement, je dois choisir entre la peste et le choléra.

Since neither one nor the other solution really suits me, I have to choose one of two bad options.

- *être assis entre deux chaises* ; *avoir le cul entre deux chaises*** ; *être assis le cul entre deux chaises*** – to be caught between two stools; to be in a difficult predicament

Literally: to be sitting between two chairs; to have the bum between two chairs; to be seated with the bum between two chairs

Il faut que je vote pour le réaménagement d'une ville, mais je suis assis entre deux chaises parce que je vis dans l'une de ces villes et travaille dans l'autre.

I have to vote for the redevelopment of one town, but I'm caught between two stools because I live in one of these towns and I work in the other.

If you have ever had to squeeze yourself in to sit between two chairs so your buttocks can feel the hard edges of both seats, you will know how uncomfortable it can be!

- *ménager la chèvre et le chou* – to keep both parties sweet*

Literally: to handle carefully the goat and the cabbage

Soucieuse de ne pas se faire d'ennemis, la direction a ménagé la chèvre et le chou.

Worried about making enemies, management have kept both parties sweet.

Do you know the brain-teaser about the boatman who wants to transport across a river a fox, a goose and a bag of beans? A French variation of this puzzle involves a goat, a wolf and a cabbage. The problem is that the boatman can carry only himself and one other item, and if he leaves the goat and the cabbage together, the goat will eat the cabbage, and if he leaves the wolf and the goat together, the wolf will eat the goat. This puzzle is the origin of this expression, which has been around for a very long time.

For those of you who are still struggling, here is the answer:

First take the goat and leave it on the far bank.

Next go back for the wolf and leave it on the far bank but bring back the goat.

Then take the cabbage to the far bank.

Finally go back for the goat and bring that across last.

Quiz 1

1. *Tiens, je ne savais pas ça ! Je me coucherai … bête ce soir !*
a) *moins*
b) *plus*
c) *aussi*

2. *Voici quelques chants populaires à connaître sur le bout des …*
a) *mains.*
b) *doigts.*
c) *ongles.*

3. *Le chef du Parti fait n'importe quoi pour avoir des votes. Quel opportunisme ! Il mange à …*
a) *toutes les mangeoires.*
b) *tous les râteliers.*
c) *tous les râteaux.*

4. *Je ne sais pas quoi choisir. Je suis assise entre deux …*
a) *tabourets.*
b) *chaises.*
c) *selles.*

5. Je suis la seule personne dans ce bureau ... même de remplir ce fichier comme il faut.
a) à
b) au
c) à la

6. Marlène a gagné un concours de dessin et un concours de mathématiques. Elle a plus d'une corde à son...
a) violon.
b) arc.
c) arche.

7. Pour vendre leur nouveau film, ils ont fait feu de ... bois : les réseaux sociaux, la publicité télévisée, les bandes annonces sur internet et les interviews à la radio.
a) tous les
b) tout
c) tout leur

8. Il connaît bien l'art de la diplomatie. Il sait ménager ...
a) la chèvre et le loup.
b) le chou et le loup.
c) la chèvre et le chou.

9. Il a besoin d'apprendre les ... du métier pour être efficace.
a) fils
b) cordons
c) ficelles

10. *Qui pourrait m'aider avec ce travail ? Tiens, ça serait tout à fait dans les ... de Marianne !*
a) *coudes*
b) *cordes*
c) *cordons*

11. *J'ai dû apprendre mon métier sur ...*
a) *le tas.*
b) *les bras.*
c) *le chat.*

12. *Je cherche à comprendre. Quelqu'un peut éclairer ...*
a) *ma lanterne ?*
b) *ma chandelle ?*
c) *mon ampoule ?*

13. *Ayant passé cinq ans au chômage, elle n'est plus dans.... Elle devra faire un stage.*
a) *le court.*
b) *la course.*
c) *la court.*

14. *En tant que ministre, il est ... de certains détails concernant les activités du gouvernement.*
a) *à la couronne*
b) *au courrier*
c) *au courant*

15. *Nous ne sommes pas riches. Il faut tirer … des ressources disponibles.*
a) *la meilleure partie*
b) *le meilleur pari*
c) *le meilleur parti*

16. *Je veux que vous vous renseigniez sur nos concurrents. …*
a) *Pouvoir, c'est savoir.*
b) *Savoir, c'est devoir.*
c) *Savoir, c'est pouvoir.*

17. *Les budgets sont restreints, donc il faut se débrouiller avec les moyens …*
a) *à bord.*
b) *d'abord.*
c) *du bord.*

18. *Je vais voter, même si je dois choisir entre la peste et …*
a) *le choléra.*
b) *le sida.*
c) *le paludisme.*

19. *« Comment vit-elle ?*
– Système … »
a) *B.*
b) *D.*
c) *Deux.*

20. *Je suis désolée, je ne peux pas vous parler des intentions de la direction. Je ne suis pas …*
a) *dans la poche.*
b) *au coup.*
c) *dans le coup.*

Answers 1

1. a
2. b
3. b
4. b
5. a
6. b
7. b
8. c
9. c
10. b

11. a
12. a
13. b
14. c
15. c
16. c
17. c
18. a
19. b
20. c

CHAPTER 2

Les premiers pas – first steps or going for it

- ***à cœur vaillant, rien d'impossible (proverbe)*** – nothing is impossible to a willing heart (proverb)

Literally: to valiant heart, nothing impossible

Avez-vous du courage ? Avez-vous de la conviction ? Pouvez-vous montrer qu'à cœur vaillant, rien n'est impossible ?

Do you have courage? Do you have conviction? Can you show that nothing is impossible to a willing heart?

This is a saying which comes from the Old French *A vaillans cuers riens impossible*. It was the motto of Jacques Cœur, a 15th century French merchant, who was one of the founders of the trade between France and the Levant. He was immensely rich and was able to help King Charles VII to reconquer the territory France had lost to England after the Battle of Agincourt. However, his wealth made him lots of enemies and he was thrown into prison after being found guilty on trumped up charges. He eventually escaped from prison but died in exile.

- ***battre le fer tant que* ou *pendant qu'il est chaud (proverbe)*** – to strike while the iron's hot (proverb)

Literally: to strike the iron while it is hot

C'est le moment opportun. Il faut battre le fer pendant qu'il est chaud !

It's the opportune moment. We must strike while the iron's hot!

We don't have many blacksmiths these days. For those who have never seen one at work, the blacksmith takes a piece of metal which is burning hot and while it is still easy to work, he strikes it with his hammer to get it into the right shape. So if you have just helped your bosses out of a very tight spot, don't let them cool off and forget your good work – now is the time to ask for that rise!

- ***donner le feu vert à quelqu'un*** – to give somebody the green light *or* the go-ahead

Literally: to give somebody the green light

La commission donne le feu vert aux négociations qui pourront commencer sans tarder.

The commission is giving the go-ahead for negotiations which can start without delay.

The first three-coloured traffic lights were introduced in France in 1933 following their introduction in Detroit. They followed the colour-coding already used on the railways. The green light gives the go-ahead.

- *franchir* ou *sauter le pas* – to take the plunge

Literally: to jump over *or* to jump the passage

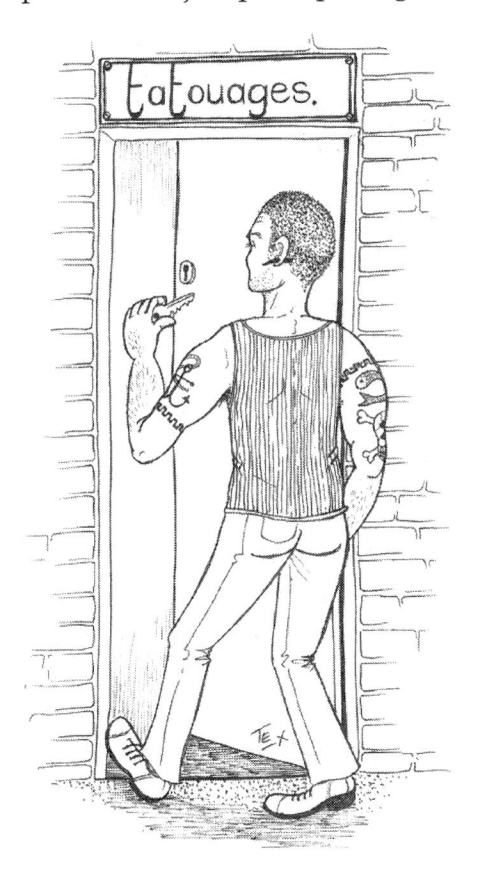

J'ai décidé de sauter le pas. Je vais ouvrir un salon de tatouage.

I've decided to take the plunge. I'm going to open a tattoo parlour.

Sauter le pas can also mean 'to die' *or* 'to kick the bucket' though it is not often used that way.

- *il n'y a que le premier pas qui coûte (proverbe)* – the first step is the hardest

Literally: there is only the first step that costs

Il n'y a que le premier pas qui coûte. Quelle que soit l'affaire, c'est le début qui est difficile. Après, ça devient moins dur.

Whatever the business, the first step is the hardest. After that, it becomes easier.

This saying is attributed to the supremely witty Marie Anne de Vichy-Chamrond, Marquise du Deffand (1697-1780), a highly intelligent and cynical woman. She had a literary salon regularly visited by her friend, Voltaire, with whom she corresponded. One day, the cardinal de Polignac was recounting the story of the Christian martyr St Denis, who, according to the legend, had been beheaded but then had picked up his head and had walked for two leagues with his head in his hands. On hearing this, the sceptical Marquise du Deffand was heard to remark, "*La distance n'y fait rien; il n'y a que le premier pas qui coûte*", 'the distance doesn't matter; it's the first step that is the hardest'.

- ***impossible n'est pas français (proverbe)*** – there's no such word as 'can't'

Literally: impossible is not French

Tout le monde m'a dit que c'était une chose impossible. Je leur ai répondu, « Impossible n'est pas français » puis je l'ai fait.

Everyone told me it can't be done. I answered, "There's no such word as 'can't'," and then I did it.

This saying is attributed to Napoléon Bonaparte. It is not an exact quotation but it is the gist of what he wrote in 1813. When le général Jean Le Marois wrote to say that it was impossible to hold the town of Magdebourg, Napoléon replied: " '*Ce n'est pas possible*', *m'écrivez-vous ! : cela n'est pas français.*"

- *mettre quelque chose sur pied* – to set something up

Literally: to put something on foot

Nous avons mis sur pied une entreprise qui fabrique des meubles.

We have set up a business which makes furniture.

- *prendre le taureau par les cornes* – to take the bull by the horns

Literally: to take the bull by the horns

Il ne sert à rien de faire des allusions. Il faut prendre le taureau par les cornes et réorganiser la société de fond en comble.

It's pointless dropping hints. You need to take the bull by the horns and shake up the organization.

- ***prendre les devants*** – to make the first move; to take the initiative

Literally: to take the fronts

N'attendez pas qu'il vous téléphone. Prenez les devants. Appelez-le !

Don't wait for him to phone you. Take the initiative. Call him!

- *se jeter à l'eau* – to take the plunge

Literally: to launch oneself into the water

Longtemps, je n'ai pas osé vous parler. Aujourd'hui, je me jette à l'eau.

For a long time, I haven't dared to speak to you. Today, I'm taking the plunge.

- ***tenter le coup**** – to have a go* or a bash at it*; to give it a try or a whirl*

Literally: to try the blow

Je ne sais pas si ça marchera, mais je te suggère de tenter le coup.

I don't know if it will work, but I suggest you give it a try.

- ***vouloir, c'est pouvoir (proverbe)*** – where there's a will, there's a way (proverb)

Literally: to want is to be able

Je suis bien décidée à réussir malgré les obstacles. Vouloir, c'est pouvoir !

I'm determined to succeed despite the obstacles. Where there's a will, there's a way!

Perdre du temps et travailler sans se fatiguer –
wasting time and taking it easy at work

- ***avoir une mentalité de fonctionnaire*** – to have a nine-to-five mentality; to have the mentality of a petty bureaucrat

Literally: to have the mentality of a state employee *or* an official

Il me faut des employés énergiques et pleins d'imagination qui soient prêts à travailler de longues heures. On ne peut pas avoir une mentalité de fonctionnaire ici !

I need energetic and imaginative employees who are ready to work long hours. You can't have a nine-to-five mentality here!

(i)

Oh to be a *fonctionnaire* in France! There are round about five and a half million lucky employees of the state in France, commonly labelled by the media as *fonctionnaires*. People working in *le secteur public* include, for example, teachers, social services staff, post office workers and railway workers. They enjoy a stability in their employment status which is the envy of workers in the private sector but they are often stereotyped as being lazy, complacent and lovers of unnecessary paperwork.

- *avoir un poil dans la main** – to be bone-idle*

Literally: to have a hair in the hand

Il préfère que les autres fassent le travail. Lui, il a un poil dans la main.

He prefers others to do the work. He's bone-idle.

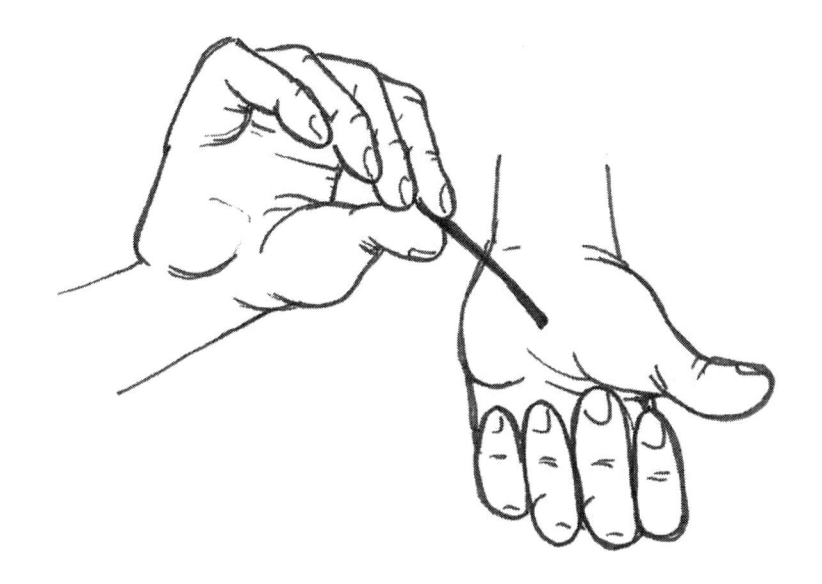

The origin of this expression, dating from the early 19th century, is not at all clear but attempts have been made to explain it. It seems that the expression has also existed in the form *avoir du poil dans la main* (to have hair rather than a hair in the hand). That would make more sense than our version because if someone never uses his hands to do work, you could imagine that hair might well have the chance to grow on the palms and a really lazy person might be too lazy to pluck it out.

You can exaggerate the level of idleness by varying the saying. For example, you could say: *ce n'est plus un poil qu'il a dans la main, mais carrément un baobab, un bâton, une canne, un bambou, un balai-brosse, un poteau télégraphique, une queue de vache* (a baobab, a stick, a cane, a bamboo, a long-handled scrubbing brush, a telegraph pole, a cow's tail) or anything else you like which is vaguely cylindrical in shape and larger than a hair.

You can also add a gesture: hold out your hand palm up and with the fingers of the other hand pull out an imaginary hair from the palm.

- *il est né fatigué* – he's bone-idle*

Literally: he was born tired

Il peut rester assis des heures à ne rien faire. Il est né fatigué.

He can be sitting doing nothing for hours on end. He's bone-idle.

- *il attend que ça lui tombe tout cuit dans le bec* – he's waiting for things to fall into his lap

Literally: he is waiting for it to fall ready-cooked into the beak

Quand tu cherches un boulot, il faut être entreprenant. Il ne faut pas attendre que ça te tombe tout cuit dans le bec.

When you're looking for a job, you have to be proactive. You can't wait for things to fall into your lap.

ⓘ

There is a variation on this saying which is less used: *il attend que les alouettes lui tombent toutes rôties dans le bec* (literally he's waiting for ready-roasted larks to fall into his beak).

- ***on n'est pas là pour enfiler des perles*** *– let's not waste time*

Literally: we are not here to thread pearls

On n'est pas là pour enfiler des perles. Allez, au travail !

Let's not waste time. To work!

- ***peigner la girafe*** *– to waste one's time doing some pointless task or other; to do nothing useful*

Literally: to comb the giraffe

J'ai vraiment l'impression de peigner la girafe à la fac. J'ai hâte de trouver un travail.

I really feel like I'm wasting my time doing nothing useful at university. I can't wait to get a job.

In 1826 the first ever giraffe was seen in France. It arrived in Marseilles then was walked all the way to Paris to the delight of massive crowds. Wouldn't it be pleasant if our expression referred to this giraffe? There is indeed a nice little anecdote about the keeper of the said giraffe at the *Jardin des Plantes* in Paris. The story goes that he was a terrible shirker and when asked what he was doing, he replied that he was combing the giraffe.

Unfortunately, this little anecdote does not appear to be true and it appears much more likely that *peigner la girafe* was in fact a euphemism for masturbating. It follows that someone who spends all his time "combing his giraffe" does not get much work done! In modern French, however, it is not considered to be a vulgar expression, only slightly colloquial, as no doubt most people using this expression are not familiar with its origin, so wouldn't imagine it to be rude.

- *se la couler douce* – to have it easy; to take it easy

Literally: to flow oneself it sweet *or* soft

Que la vie est belle pour moi ! Je me la coule douce sur la plage pendant que mes employés font tout le travail au bureau.

What a wonderful life it is for me! I take it easy on the beach while my employees do all the work in the office.

- *se tourner les pouces* – to twiddle one's thumbs; to spend time idly doing nothing

Literally: to turn one's thumbs

Ce n'est pas en vous tournant les pouces que vous êtes devenu riche.

You didn't get rich twiddling your thumbs.

Balzac used the form *tourner ses pouces* in 1834. By 1893 this had become *se tourner les pouces*. Long before this, we have the nice turn of phrase *les poulces à la ceinture* (thumbs hooked over a belt) to convey laziness.

Make sure you get the vowel sound right in the word *pouces*. If you pronounce it like *puces,* you will be telling people you are twiddling your flees!

Quiz 2

1. « *Il travaille dur pendant son stage ?*
– Tu veux rire ! Il passe son temps à … la girafe ! »
a) *brosser*
b) *peigner*
c) *chasser*

2. *C'est un vrai fainéant. Il a … dans la main.*
a) *un poêle*
b) *un poil*
c) *une poêle*

3. *J'ai pris ma décision. Je ne suis pas sûr de réussir, mais je vais me jeter …*
a) *en l'air.*
b) *par terre.*
c) *à l'eau.*

4. *J'ai une idée pour une nouvelle entreprise et je vais essayer de la mettre … pied cette année.*
a) *à*
b) *sur*
c) *sous*

5. Il a du courage et de la détermination. Il dit toujours : « À cœur ... , rien d'impossible ! »
a) *courageux*
b) *vaillant*
c) *vainquant*

6. Il ne s'intéresse qu'à ses vacances et à la stabilité de son poste. Il a une mentalité de ...
a) *fonctionnaire.*
b) *facteur.*
c) *fonceur.*

7. Il faut prendre des mesures immédiates. Prenez le taureau par ... !
a) *les cornes*
b) *les oreilles*
c) *la queue*

8. Jeanne est paresseuse de nature. Elle est ... fatiguée.
a) *arrivée*
b) *venue*
c) *née*

9. Nous devons agir immédiatement ! Battons le ... tant qu'il est chaud !
a) *fer*
b) *feu*
c) *ver*

10. « J'aimerais quitter mon poste et fonder ma propre entreprise, mais j'ai peur.
– Oui, il n'y a que … qui coûte. »
a) *le premier pas*
b) *la première passe*
c) *la première patte*

11. *Je ne vous ai pas embauchés pour que vous vous tourniez les …*
a) *puces.*
b) *pouces.*
c) *pieds.*

12. *N'attendez pas qu'il vous écrive. Prenez …*
a) *le devant.*
b) *les devants.*
c) *l'avant.*

13. *Vous perdez du temps ! On n'est pas là pour … des perles.*
a) *enlacer*
b) *ennuyer*
c) *enfiler*

14. *La détermination est la garantie de la réussite. …*
a) *Pouvoir, c'est vouloir !*
b) *Vouloir, c'est savoir !*
c) *Vouloir, c'est pouvoir !*

15. *Je veux commencer les travaux tout de suite, mais je dois attendre que la mairie me donne ...*
a) *le feu.*
b) *le feu rouge.*
c) *le feu vert.*

16. *Je suis sur le point d'acheter une boulangerie, mais j'ai quelques questions avant de ... le pas.*
a) *passer*
b) *monter*
c) *sauter*

17. *Impossible n'est pas ...*
a) *français.*
b) *suisse.*
c) *belge.*

18. *Pendant que le patron est en vacances, je me la coule ...*
a) *gentil.*
b) *sympa.*
c) *douce.*

19. *Prends un risque. Tente ...*
a) *un coup.*
b) *le coup.*
c) *les coups.*

20. *Il ne fait rien pour trouver un boulot. Il attend que ça lui tombe tout cuit ...*
a) *sur la tête.*
b) *sur le crâne.*
c) *dans le bec.*

Answers 2

1. b
2. b
3. c
4. b
5. b
6. a
7. a
8. c
9. a
10. a

11. b
12. b
13. c
14. c
15. c
16. c
17. a
18. c
19. b
20. c

CHAPTER 3

Travailler dur – working hard

- *arriver* **ou** *réussir à la force du poignet* – to manage to do something; to succeed by sheer hard work *or* by the sweat of one's brow

Literally: to manage *or* succeed by the force of the wrist *or* the cuff

Si vous avez beaucoup d'ambition et d'énergie, vous pouvez arriver à la force du poignet.

If you have lots of ambition and drive, you can succeed by sheer hard work.

It might seem a little strange that the wrist should be seen as something containing strength. Normally we would think of the clenched fist as being the symbol of strength. If we look at the French words for fist, *le poing*, and the word for the cuff or wrist, *le poignet*, we get some clue as to the origin of the expression. *Poignet* is in fact the diminutive of *poing* (i.e. a little fist). *Le poing* and *le poignet* are right next to each other on the body and they sound remarkably similar, so it is not so surprising that the idea of strength might have slipped from one to the other (no doubt helped along by the old French word *poigne* (f) which also meant cuff but which figuratively meant 'the strength of the fist', 'energy' and 'firmness').

- ***avoir fort à faire (littéraire)*** – to have one's work cut out

Literally: to have much to do (literary)

Nous aurons fort à faire si nous voulons finir avant les grandes vacances.

We will have our work cut out if we want to finish before the summer holidays.

The normal translation for the word *fort* is 'strong' but in a literary style it means the same as *beaucoup*.

- *avoir du pain sur la planche** – to have one's work cut out

Literally: to have some bread on the plank

Le lancement est prévu pour fin mars. On a du pain sur la planche si on veut être prêts.

The launch is scheduled for the end of March. We've got our work cut out if we want to be ready.

Over the years, the meaning of this expression has changed. In the 19th century, in the days when bread stayed fresh for a few days and was stored on an overhead shelf, *une planche*, it meant 'to be able to live without working', as there was enough food stored away to be going on with.

But how did it change to its present meaning of having lots of work to do? This isn't very clear but Claude Duneton makes a suggestion in his excellent book *La Puce à l'oreille*. He thinks it is partly thanks to the slang expression dating from the 18th century, **manger le pain du roi**, 'to eat the king's bread'. If you were joining the army or had a long prison stretch in front of you, you were provided with free bread rations. Also, in a court of law, the bench for the accused was called *la planche au pain* because the court gave out long sentences resulting in the receipt of lots of free bread. This use has disappeared from modern French.

The modern day meaning, dating from the time of the First World War, probably has more to do with a baker who has started to prepare his loaves and has put them on a shelf to prove but has not yet baked them, so he still has a lot of work ahead of him.

- *c'est en forgeant qu'on devient forgeron (proverbe)* – practice makes perfect (proverb)

Literally: it is by forging that one becomes blacksmith

Mes premières tentatives à la poterie étaient désastreuses, mais je me suis dit : « C'est en forgeant qu'on devient forgeron ».

My first attempts at pottery were disastrous, but I told myself, "Practice makes perfect".

- *ce n'est pas du gâteau** – it's no picnic*

Literally: it is not cake

Travailler dehors en hiver, c'est pas du gâteau !

Working out of doors in winter is no picnic!

(i)

You don't have to use this expression in the negative: ***c'est du gâteau*** means 'it's a piece of cake' or 'it's a doddle'. However, the related expression, ***c'est pas de la tarte*****, meaning 'it's no joke' or 'it's no easy matter', is only used in the negative. To pronounce it like a real French person, shorten the *de*: *C'est pas d'la tarte*.

- ***donner un coup de collier*** – to put one's back into it; to produce a short and intense burst of effort; to make a big effort

Literally: to give a blow of collar

Nous devons donner un sacré coup de collier pour finir à temps.

We really need to put our backs into it to get it finished in time.

This expression has nothing to do with *un collier*, 'necklace', worn as jewellery but rather is more to do with beasts of burden. Back in the days when horses were used to plough the fields, they wore harnesses with *un collier*, 'a collar', around the neck. If there was a particularly difficult obstacle to overcome, the horse had to make a great effort and pull hard on its collar.

- ***en mettre un coup*** – to really put one's back into it

Literally: to put a blow of it

Allez ! Il faudra en mettre un coup si on veut finir de décharger ces camions avant la fin de la journée.

Come on! We're going to have to really put our backs into it if we're going to unload these lorries before the end of the day.

- ***être dur à l'ouvrage*** – to be a tireless worker

Literally: to be hard at the work

Je le recommande. Il est fort et dur à l'ouvrage.

I recommend him. He is a strong and tireless worker.

- *faire des pieds et des mains (pour obtenir quelque chose)* – to move heaven and earth *or* to bend over backwards (to get something)

Literally: to do with feet and hands (to obtain something)

Nous allons faire des pieds et des mains pour y arriver.

We are going to move heaven and earth to succeed.

This expression dates from the 19th century. If you really want to get something done, you need to put all your energy into it and if your hands alone don't get the job done, then use your feet too!

A more direct translation of the English expression 'to move heaven and earth' also exists: ***remuer ciel et terre***.

- ***gagner son pain à la sueur de son front*** – to earn a living by the sweat of one's brow

Literally: to earn one's bread by the sweat of one's brow.

Je ne veux pas vivre grâce aux allocations de chômage. Je veux gagner mon pain à la sueur de mon front.

I don't want to live on unemployment benefits. I want to earn a living by the sweat of my brow.

The Bible is the origin of this expression. Genesis chapter 3, verse 19 reads: *"Tu mangeras ton pain à la sueur de ton visage jusqu'à ce que tu retournes dans la terre d'où tu as été tiré."* 'In the sweat of thy face shalt thou eat bread, till thou return unto the ground; for out of it wast thou taken.' In other words, you need to work hard to earn your living until you drop dead!

- *je vais lui montrer de quel bois je me chauffe** – I'll show him what I'm made of; I'm going to show him what I'm capable of; I'm not going down without a fight

Literally: I'm going to show him with what wood I warm myself

« *Montrez que vous êtes capable de mener à bien ce projet ambitieux.*

– Oui, je vais leur montrer de quel bois je me chauffe ! »

"Show that you are capable of seeing this ambitious project through."

"Yes, I'll show them what I'm made of!"

This expression dates back to the 16th century, long before central heating, to a time when people knew a thing or two about which type of wood produced the brightest heat when burnt.

- ***ne pas avoir les deux pieds dans le même sabot*** – to be energetic and dynamic

Literally: not to have two feet in the same clog

Elle s'apprête à relever de nouveaux défis. Elle n'a pas les deux pieds dans le même sabot.

She's getting ready to take up new challenges. She's energetic and dynamic.

Though this expression might sound like an ancient one, as it refers to clogs which no-one wears any more, in fact it only appeared in the 20th century. Imagine a woman who has managed to force both feet into the same shoe: she wouldn't be moving very far without falling flat on her face!

You don't have to use this saying in the negative. You can also say, "**Elle a les pieds dans le même sabot**", meaning 'she is incapable of acting' or 'she is passive and without initiative' but you are more likely to meet it in the negative used as a compliment.

- *métro, boulot, dodo* – the daily routine of commuting, work then bed; work, work, work!

Literally: underground, work, sleep

Mon mari travaille à la Défense. Pour lui, c'est métro, boulot, dodo.

My husband works in Paris's financial district. For him, it's work, work, work!

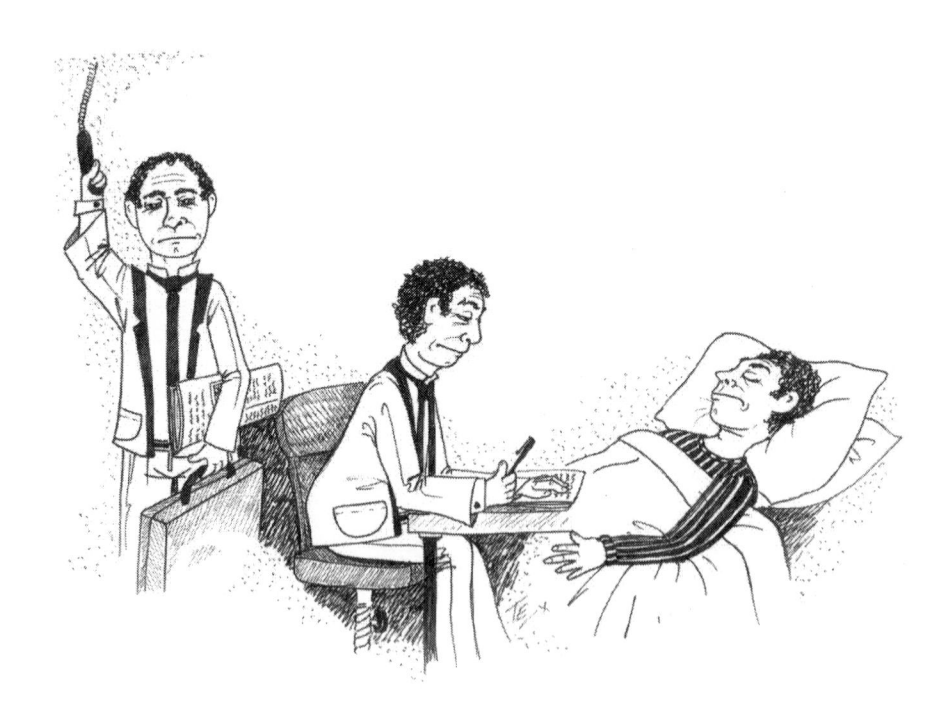

This saying has come from an abbreviation of the last line of a poem written by Pierre Béarn in 1951. It comes from his collection *Couleurs d'usine* (Factory Colours).

"*Au déboulé garçon pointe ton numéro
Pour gagner ainsi le salaire
D'un morne jour utilitaire
Métro, boulot, bistro, mégots, dodo, zéro*"

'Rush in boy punch your number
Thus to earn the salary
Of a dreary utilitarian day
Metro, work, bistro, cigs, sleep, zero'

Dodo is baby language for 'sleep'. **Fais dodo !** – Go to sleep!

- ***mettre le paquet*** – to spare no expense; to pull out all the stops

Literally: to put the packet

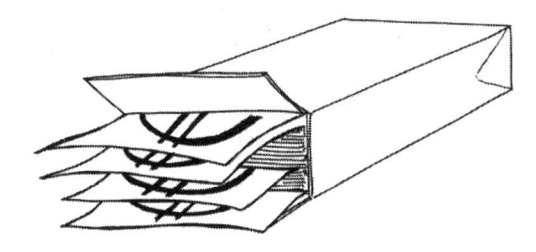

Je dois dire qu'elle a fait tout ce qui était possible. Elle a vraiment mis le paquet.

I have to say that she did everything possible. She really pulled out all the stops.

The origin of this expression is uncertain but it might come from the South-West of France where the word *paquet* meant 'a wad of notes', so it meant 'to spend a lot of money on something'.

- ***mettre les bouchées doubles*** – to work twice as hard; to work quicker; to put on a spurt

Literally: to put the double mouthfuls

Vous avez un bulletin mensuel à écrire pour jeudi. Hier vous n'avez rien fait, donc aujourd'hui vous avez intérêt à mettre les bouchées doubles.

You've got a monthly report to write for Thursday. Yesterday you did nothing, so today you'd be well advised to put on a spurt.

If you are in a hurry and want to clear your plate of food, the quickest way to accomplish this would be to double the quantity of food you put on your fork; hence **mettre les bouchées doubles**. If you really want to hurry people along, you could even tell them to "***mettre les bouchées triples***".

- *se donner un mal de chien pour faire quelque chose* – to try really hard *or* to bend over backwards* *or* to bust a gut** to do something

Literally: to give oneself a dog's pain to do something

Il s'est donné un mal de chien pour répondre à tous les messages qu'il a reçus.

He tried really hard to reply to all the messages he received.

These days we tend to think of a dog as being man's best friend and being loved and cossetted by its owner. Unfortunately, over the years the dog has suffered badly at the hands of humans and the phrase "*de chien*" refers to pain and difficulty.

- *se jeter à corps perdu dans une entreprise* **ou** *la mêlée* – to throw oneself wholeheartedly into a venture *or* into the fray

Literally: to throw oneself with lost body into a venture *or* the fray

Il se jette à corps perdu dans les entreprises les plus risquées sans penser à sa famille.

He throws himself into the riskiest of businesses without thinking of his family.

Perdu is from the verb *perdre*, 'to lose'. Imagine a young volunteer throwing himself headlong into a bloody battle without any thought for the risk he is running to his poor body. It's as if his head is no longer attached to his body as he gets carried away by the urge to commit. His body is as good as lost. The origin of this expression is not known but it has the meaning of throwing oneself into something, risking one's own life without holding back.

- *suer sang et eau* – to sweat blood (and tears)

Literally: to sweat blood and water

Vous devez suer sang et eau pour compléter ce projet à temps.

You must sweat blood and tears to get this project completed in time.

- *un travail de longue haleine* – a long job

Literally: a job of long breath

Le développement d'un médicament est un travail de longue haleine.

The development of a medicine is a long job.

- ***y mettre du sien*** – to do one's bit; to make an effort; to be understanding

Literally: to put of one's own there

Si l'on veut s'entendre, il faut que chacun y mette du sien.

If we all want to get along, everyone has to make an effort.

You would have to change the word "*sien*" to agree with the person who is doing their bit, so:

y mettre du sien – to do one's *or* his *or* her bit

y mettre du mien – to do my bit

y mettre du tien ou *du vôtre* – to do your bit

y mettre du nôtre – to do our bit

y mettre du leur – to do their bit

In the 12th century, the noun *sien* meant 'wealth' or 'possessions', so ***y mettre du sien*** meant 'to contribute wealth or possessions'. It is from this that we get the idea in the modern expression of an act of self-sacrifice or doing something which costs you personally. Figuratively, it might just be that you are making a personal effort to help out and the cost might have nothing to do with money.

Quiz 3

1. *Si nous voulons être prêts avant demain, nous avons ... à faire.*
a) *fier*
b) *fort*
c) *fou*

2. *Je suis sûr que je trouverai bientôt un emploi, car je suis ... à l'ouvrage.*
a) *dû*
b) *dur*
c) *dupe*

3. *La première fois que j'ai essayé de faire du repassage, j'ai brûlé la chemise, mais je me suis dit : ...*
a) « *C'est en forgeant qu'on devient forgeron* ».
b) « *C'est en cuisant qu'on devient cuistot* ».
c) « *C'est en fournissant qu'on devient fournisseur* ».

4. *Debout les gars ! Réveillez-vous ! Il va falloir ... mettre un coup.*
a) *le*
b) *à*
c) *en*

5. *Je suis arrivé par mon seul travail, à la force ...*
a) *du poing.*
b) *de la poignée.*
c) *du poignet.*

6. *Il faut un dernier coup de ... et me voilà prêt.*
a) *col*
b) *collier*
c) *colle*

7. *Je n'ai pas de temps libre cet après-midi ; j'ai du pain sur ...*
a) *le plancher.*
b) *le plafond.*
c) *la planche.*

8. *Ne soyez pas paresseux ! Il faut gagner son pain à la sueur de ... !*
a) *son dos*
b) *ses aisselles*
c) *son front*

9. *Lorsqu'il voit une nouvelle opportunité, il s'y jette à corps ...*
a) *pendu.*
b) *perduré.*
c) *perdu.*

10. *Pendant des années, elle a fait ... pour recevoir une promotion.*
a) *des pieds et des mains*
b) *des mains et des pieds*
c) *mains et pieds*

11. « *Travailler dans un centre d'appels, c'est agréable ?*
– *Croyez-moi, c'est pas …* »
a) *du gâteau.*
b) *un biscuit.*
c) *du pain.*

12. *Depuis ma promotion, ce n'est que …*
a) *métro, boulot, dodo.*
b) *boulot, dodo, métro.*
c) *dodo, métro, boulot.*

13. *Je la trouve très énergique. Elle n'a pas les deux pieds dans …*
a) *la même chaussure.*
b) *le même soulier.*
c) *le même sabot.*

14. « *Montrez-leur de quoi vous êtes capable !*
– *Oui, je vais leur montrer de quel … je me chauffe !* »
a) *fuel*
b) *gaz*
c) *bois*

15. *Les noces étaient superbes. On a vraiment mis …*
a) *le paquebot.*
b) *la pâquerette.*
c) *le paquet.*

16. *Il y a tellement à faire avant demain. Il faut mettre ...*
a) *les bouchées doubles.*
b) *les grandes bouchées.*
c) *les bouches doubles.*

17. *Il s'est donné un mal de ..., mais ça ne marche toujours pas.*
a) *chat*
b) *chien*
c) *cheval*

18. *J'ai sué ... pour finir ce projet.*
a) *encre et eau*
b) *sang et encre*
c) *sang et eau*

19. *Repeindre la tour Eiffel, c'est un travail de ...*
a) *large haleine.*
b) *longue haleine.*
c) *grand haltère.*

20. *J'ai dû y mettre du ...*
a) *sien.*
b) *mien.*
c) *tien.*

Answers 3

1.	b	11.	a
2.	b	12.	a
3.	a	13.	c
4.	c	14.	c
5.	c	15.	c
6.	b	16.	a
7.	c	17.	b
8.	c	18.	c
9.	c	19.	b
10.	a	20.	b

CHAPTER 4

Les problèmes – Problems

- *avoir beau faire quelque chose* – no matter what one does; whatever one does; to do something in vain

Literally: to have beautiful doing something

On avait beau protester, sa décision était sans appel.

It was no use protesting; his decision was final.

- *avoir* **ou** *faire deux poids (et) deux mesures* – to have double standards

Literally: to have *or* to make two weights (and) two measures

Je trouve épouvantable qu'on ait eu droit à un système « deux poids deux mesures ».

I think it is appalling there were double standards.

This is a bit of a strange expression and it is hard to get to the bottom of it. What it seems to come down to is that if you take two similar things and you judge one by its weight and the other by its length, or use any two different sets of measurements, you are applying different criteria; hence the injustice. It appears to date back to Voltaire in the 18th century.

- *avoir quelque chose* ou *quelqu'un sur les bras** – to have something *or* somebody on one's hands; to be landed with something *or* stuck with something *or* somebody

Literally: to have something *or* somebody on the arms

Je vais vendre nos surplus sur leboncoin. Je ne veux pas qu'ils nous restent sur les bras.

I'm going to sell our surplus stock on *leboncoin.fr* (French equivalent of eBay). I don't want to be stuck with it.

- ***ça me fait une belle jambe ! (ironique)*** – a fat lot of good that does me!*

Literally: that makes me a fine leg (ironic)

Il dit qu'il me payera en janvier. Ça me fait une belle jambe ! Je dois acheter des cadeaux avant Noël !

He says he'll pay me in January. A fat lot of good that does me! I need to buy presents before Christmas!

At one time in history, men wore short tunics with leggings which showed off their shapely calves, and of course, the more vain men would consider it important to show off their legs. This expression refers back to that fashion and makes fun of it. Because it is used ironically, it could be said to mean 'it doesn't even make me a beautiful leg', i.e. it is useless.

- **c'est le bouquet !*** – that takes the biscuit!*; that's just great!(ironic)

Literally: it is the bouquet

Et voilà que maintenant il commence à pleuvoir. Çà, c'est le bouquet !

And now it's starting to rain. That's just great!

Dating from the late 18th century, *le bouquet* referred to the climax of a fireworks display when all of the best rockets appeared in the sky to rapturous applause, oohs and ahs. It originally meant 'the best there could be' but is now used ironically, so means 'the worst that could happen'.

ⓘ

A film by Jeanne Labrune called "*C'est le bouquet !*" was released in 2002. It is a light comedy in which an ill-advised early-morning phone call from an old friend starts a string of unfortunate events, and a bouquet of flowers, sent as an apology, gets delivered to the wrong address and causes a rumpus. As is often the case, there is an obvious play on words in the title – *le bouquet* having both a literal and a figurative meaning.

- *c'est trop beau pour être vrai* – it's too good to be true

Literally: it is too beautiful *or* good to be true

- *ce serait trop beau !* – that would be too much to hope for!

Literally: that would be too beautiful *or* good

J'ai entendu dire que nos nouveaux locaux commerciaux seront prêts avant la fin du mois, mais ce serait trop beau.

I have heard that our new business premises will be ready before the end of the month, but that would be too much to hope for.

ⓘ

There's a wonderful old song called "*C'est trop beau*" sung by the French Corsican singer Tino Rossi (1907-1983) which is well worth listening to and will soon have you dancing with your loved-one around the kitchen floor! The words are easy to sing along to (you can find them on the Figure out French website). On hearing the tune, it sounds wonderfully romantic but when you pay the lyrics a little attention, you will realize he is saying that their love affair is too good to be true and probably won't last, so maybe it is not such a good one to sing to your beloved after all!

Rossi, a real heart-throb, was immensely popular in the mid-20th century, especially in the 1930s and 40s as both a singer and an actor. The Americans coined the term "Latin lover" for him and he was the romantic idol of millions of women around the world. Put "Tino Rossi *C'est trop beau*" into a search engine and enjoy!

- *changer de crémerie** – to take one's business elsewhere; to push off* somewhere else

Literally: to change dairy shop

J'ai fait mes affaires avec vous pendant trente ans, mais j'ai été si mal traité récemment que j'ai décidé de changer de crémerie.

I have done business with you for thirty years, but I have been treated so badly recently that I have decided to take my business elsewhere.

Though the word *crémerie* does mean 'a shop which sells dairy products', in the 19th century *la crémerie* referred to a type of restaurant or bar which sold both food and alcohol. It is likely that heated arguments, fuelled by the over-consumption of wine, might well have led to customers deciding quite regularly to take their custom elsewhere. The word *crémerie* by extension came to mean 'an establishment' and then quite simply 'any place'.

ⓘ

You can also spell the word *crémerie* with a grave accent: *crèmerie*.

- *chercher la petite bête* – to split hairs; to nit-pick*; to be extremely meticulous; to do one's best to find mistakes

Literally: to look for the small insect

J'ai beau faire du mieux que je peux, mon chef ne fait que chercher la petite bête.

It doesn't matter how hard I try, my boss does nothing but nit-pick.

Before the advent of chemical treatments for lice, the only way to get rid of the little blighters was to search carefully for them then meticulously pull the unwanted creatures away from the hair to which they were firmly attached. Someone willing to look for the little insects was looking for problems; hence the metaphor.

ⓘ

There is a very similar expression, **chercher des poux dans la tête de quelqu'un*** (literally to look for lice in somebody's head), which means 'to try to make trouble for somebody'.

- ***être dans le pétrin** ou *la panade*** – to be in a mess* *or* a fix* *or* a jam*; to be in a sticky* *or* embarrassing situation

Literally: to be in the kneading trough *or* the bread soup

Si nous ne parvenons pas à résoudre ces problèmes, nous sommes vraiment dans le pétrin.

If we cannot solve these problems, we are really in a mess.

In the bread-making trade, *le pétrin* is the name for the large container with a mechanical arm which kneads the bread. The dough in the trough is sticky and if you fell in it, you'd really have trouble getting back out of it again!

- *faire faux bond à quelqu'un* – to let somebody down; to leave somebody in the lurch

Literally: to do somebody a false bounce

Le système leur a fait faux bond et cela leur a coûté cher.

The system let them down and that cost them dearly.

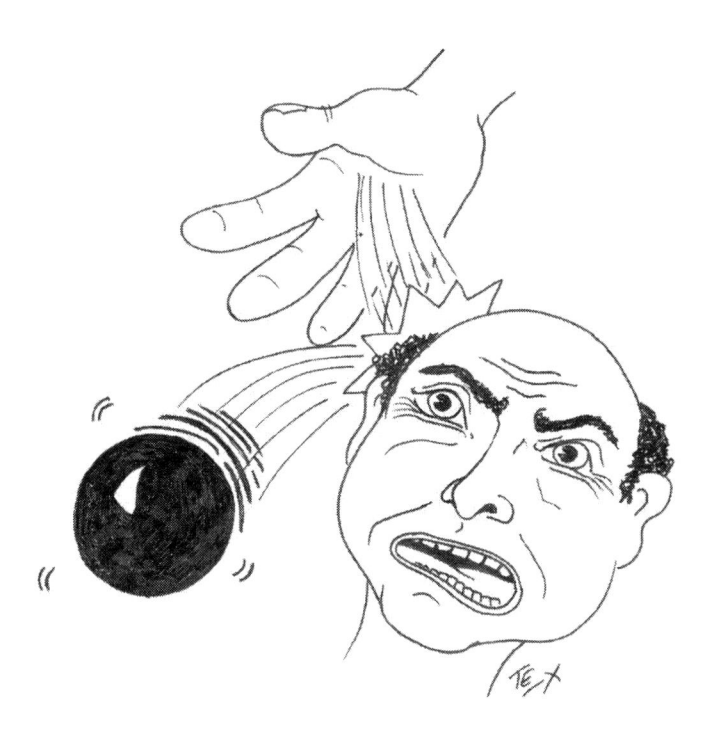

This expression dates back to the 16th century to the game of *jeu de paume* (palm game or real tennis). *Le jeu de paume* was the precursor of tennis. It was played indoors, originally using the palm of the hand to hit the ball rather than a racket. **Faire faux bond** meant that the ball bounced in an unexpected way, perhaps because the ground wasn't perfectly flat. Figuratively, a person is expecting one thing but something different and disappointing happens instead.

- *ficher tout par terre** – to mess everything up

Literally: to put everything on the ground

J'étais sur ma lancée, et puis mon mobile a sonné et ça a tout fichu par terre.

I was in full flow, and then my mobile rang and messed everything up.

ⓘ

Notice the irregular past tense form of *ficher*, *fichu*, which has developed by analogy with the past participle of *foutre* which is *foutu*.

This expression using *ficher* is a mild colloquial expression but there is a more vulgar variation: *ça fout tout par terre***, which is more akin to the ubiquitous English expression 'that f***s it all up'. There is a very interesting discussion on the website Wordreference.com about exactly how rude the verb *foutre* is. The general consensus is that it is very vulgar and not to be used in front of children (or for that matter your boss). Some idioms using *foutre* are indeed very rude. That being said, there are some expressions in common usage employing the verb *foutre*, such as **je m'en fous****, 'I couldn't give a damn'**, which are not considered vulgar. However, beware!

- **jeter un pavé dans la mare** – to set the cat among the pigeons

Literally: to throw a cobblestone in the pond

Quand notre directeur nous a révélé ses projets pour l'année qui vient, il a jeté un pavé dans la mare.

When our manager revealed to us his plans for the coming year, he set the cat among the pigeons.

- *laisser en plan** – to abandon *or* drop *or* ditch* (a project); to leave in the lurch *or* high and dry (a person)

Literally: to leave in plan

A cause de la politique de rigueur du gouvernement, nous avons dû laisser en plan notre projet d'agrandissement.

Because of the government's austerity measures, we have had to abandon our expansion plans.

Alain Rey explains that the noun *plan* comes from the verb *planter*, 'to plant'. It was first spelled *plant* with a t. The 15th century writer Villon used *en plant* to mean 'in prison' (if you are planted in the ground, you can't move). The later expression, dating from the 19th century, *laisser en plan*, picks up this idea of being prevented from moving. Maybe you have been abandoned and are stuck where you are or perhaps your plans are unable to get off the ground.

- *lever* **ou** *soulever un lièvre* – to hit on a problem; to notice a problem before other people do

Literally: to lift a hare

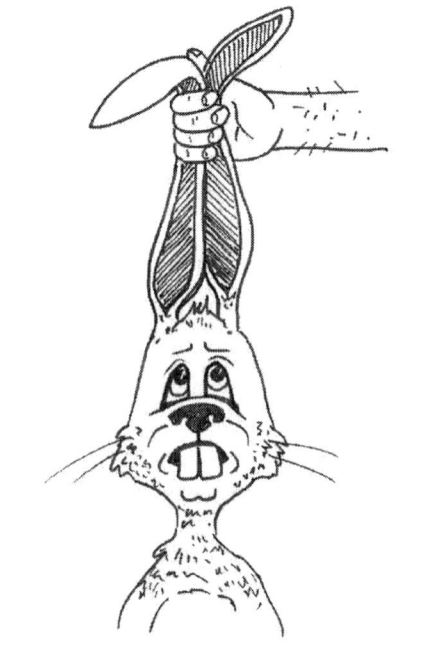

Là vous avez levé un sacré lièvre. Qu'est-ce qu'on va faire pour résoudre le problème ?

There you've hit on one hell of a snag. What are we going to do to solve the problem?

This expression comes directly from hunting and has been around since the 17th century. If you are out hunting and come across a hare, you have been surprised by something unexpected. A snag is a problem which has been well hidden before it is stumbled upon, just as a hare lies hidden before it darts out in front of you. The hunter with the best chance of shooting the hare is the first one to startle the animal; hence the idea of being the first to notice a problem.

- *mettre des bâtons dans les roues* – to put a spanner in the works

Literally: to put some sticks in the wheels

Tout avançait bien, puis on a mis en place de nouveaux règlements et ça nous a mis des bâtons dans les roues.

Everything was progressing well, then they brought in new rules and that put a spanner in the works.

- *se faire pigeonner***; *se faire prendre* **ou** *passer pour un pigeon** – to be taken for a ride**; to be had*; to be duped

Literally: to have oneself "pigeonned"; to have oneself taken for a pigeon

J'étais bien obligé de reconnaître que je m'étais fait pigeonner quand j'ai compris que mon assistant particulier avait disparu avec le contenu de mon compte bancaire.

I had to admit that I'd been had when I saw that my personal assistant had disappeared with the contents of my bank account.

This expression has evolved in an interesting way. You have to follow it through several stages. Let's start with a little bird called *la huppe*, the hoopoe, which has a crest on the top of its head. In fact the French word *huppe* means 'crest' and that is why the bird was thus named. *Déhupper* contracted to *duper* meant 'to cut the crest off'. *Plumer* meant 'to pluck' and also, figuratively, 'to fleece' someone (being stripped of one's goods is like being plucked). So *plumer* and *duper* both meant 'to remove the feathers' and both took on the figurative meaning of 'to dupe' or 'to fleece' someone. Someone who lets himself be robbed is considered a dupe or a fool.

So where does the pigeon come into this? Well, a pigeon is a much more common bird than a hoopoe and it was often plucked, so it took the place of *la huppe* in this expression. *Se faire pigeonner* is to get oneself plucked, or as we now say, "to be duped".

- *se plaindre pour un oui (ou) pour un non* – to complain over the slightest thing

Literally: to complain for a yes (or) for a no

Les clients m'énervent. Ils se plaignent toujours pour un oui pour un non !

The customers annoy me. They are always complaining over the slightest thing!

Identifier ses priorités – prioritizing

- *de premier plan* – key

Literally: of first plane; of foreground

Dans le brassage de bière, l'eau est un ingrédient de premier plan.

In the brewing of beer, water is a key ingredient.

If you look at a classical painting, you can identify a foreground, a middle ground and a background. A character placed in the foreground is *au premier plan*; in the middle ground is *au second plan*; and in the background is *à l'arrière-plan*. By 1803 these terms were also being applied to the stage in a theatre. The more important characters act at the front of the stage, *au premier plan*, and the less important roles are relegated to nearer the back of the stage. From this concrete use, the development into a figurative expression is easy to understand: someone or something which is *de premier plan* must be of prime importance.

- *mettre au premier plan* – to consider as the most important issue

Literally: to put in the first plane; to put in the foreground

Nous continuons de mettre au premier plan le bien-être de nos employés.

We continue to consider as the most important issue the well-being of our employees.

- *mettre au deuxième* ou *second plan* – to consider something as of secondary importance

Literally: to put at second plane; to put in the middle ground

Dans notre politique d'embauche, les compétences ont été mises au deuxième plan. C'est l'attitude qui compte.

In our employment policy, skills are considered as of secondary importance. It is attitude which counts.

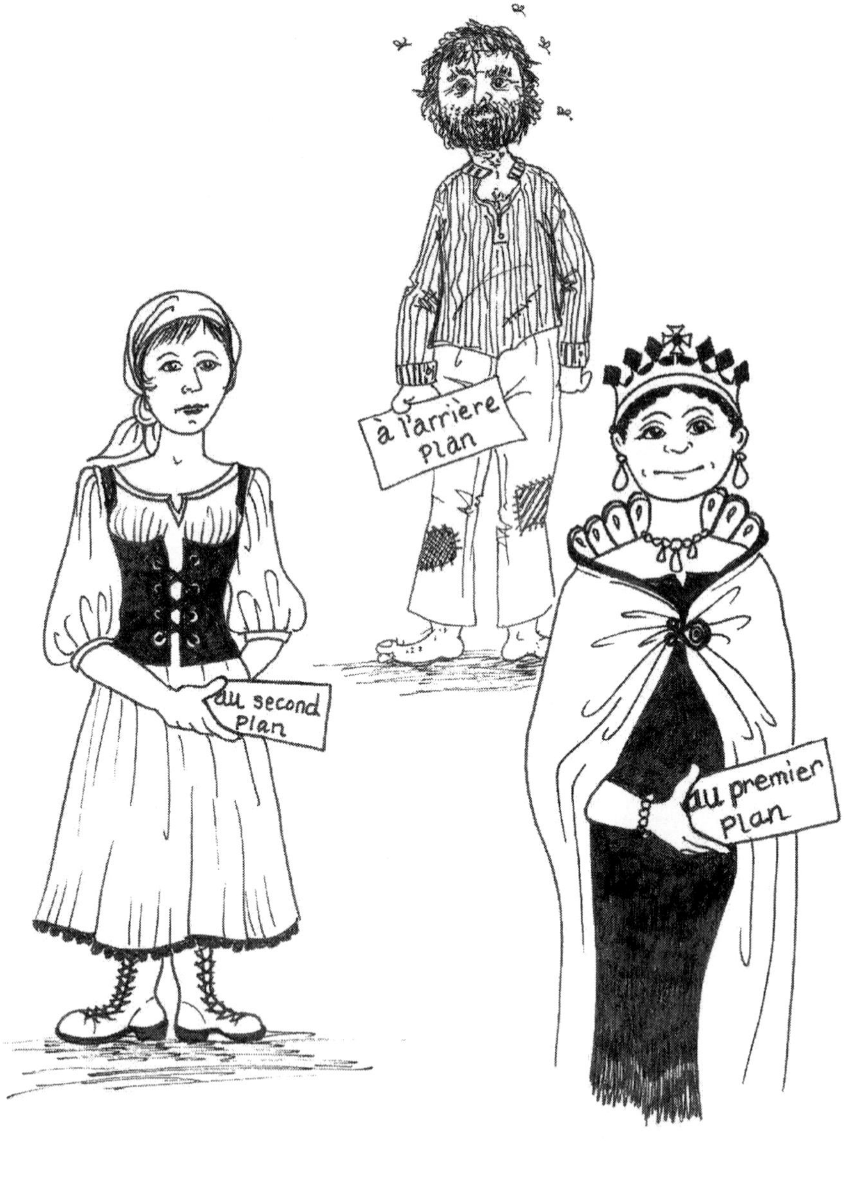
à l'arrière
plan
au second
plan
au premier
plan

Quiz 4

1. *Il m'a mis des ... dans les roues.*
a) *bateaux*
b) *baguettes*
c) *bâtons*

2. *Il faut trouver une autre technique parce qu'on a levé ...*
a) *un lapin.*
b) *un lièvre.*
c) *un civet de lièvre.*

3. *Il m'a dit qu'il n'allait pas m'abandonner, mais il m'a laissé ...*
a) *en haut.*
b) *sur terre.*
c) *en plan.*

4. *Je crois que je suis un patron tout à fait raisonnable. Je ne cherche pas la petite ...*
a) *bête.*
b) *lente.*
c) *puce.*

5. Je mets l'âge du candidat au ... plan. Ce n'est pas très important.
a) *premier*
b) *secondaire*
c) *deuxième*

6. Votre santé m'est très importante. Je la mets ...
a) *au premier plan.*
b) *au dernier plan.*
c) *au premier plant.*

7. Il a dit que c'était aux frais de la maison mais moi j'ai cru que c'était ... pour être vrai.
a) *trop joli*
b) *trop beau*
c) *très bien*

8. Je ne suis pas libre ce soir. J'ai les enfants ...
a) *sous les bras.*
b) *sous les mains.*
c) *sur les bras.*

9. J'ai eu ... téléphoner, il n'a pas voulu me parler.
a) *bel*
b) *beau*
c) *bien*

10. *Ce n'est pas juste. Ils font deux … deux mesures.*
a) *pois*
b) *points*
c) *poids*

11. *Le directeur a un rôle …*
a) *de premier plan.*
b) *de plant.*
c) *de premier plant.*

12. *Je travaillais paisiblement seul à la maison, puis ma femme est rentrée avec les trois enfants et ça m'a fichu tout …*
a) *sur la terre.*
b) *par terre.*
c) *en terre.*

13. *Il faut être fiable. Nous ne devons pas leur faire faux …*
a) *pas.*
b) *bond.*
c) *départ.*

14. *Je suis très déçu du service que nous avons eu dans ce restaurant. Je vais changer de …*
a) *boulangerie.*
b) *crème.*
c) *crémerie.*

15. Le nouveau patron, voulant tout changer, a jeté … dans la mare.
a) *un pâté*
b) *un pavé*
c) *une pierre*

16. Il dit qu'il peut me donner un coup de main demain. Ça me fait une … jambe ! J'ai besoin de lui aujourd'hui !
a) *jolie*
b) *belle*
c) *longue*

17. Je trouve M. Boyer très exigeant. Il se plaint …
a) *pour un oui pour un non.*
b) *par un oui par un non.*
c) *pour un non pour un oui.*

18. Je travaille dehors aujourd'hui, et regarde, il neige. Çà, c'est … !
a) *le bouquet*
b) *la botte*
c) *le biscuit*

19. Je suis au chômage et profondément endetté. C'est vrai que je suis dans …
a) *la confiture.*
b) *le pâté.*
c) *le pétrin.*

20. « On t'a escroqué ?
– Oui, je me suis fait … »
a) *canarder.*
b) *moutonner.*
c) *pigeonner.*

Answers 4

1. c
2. b
3. c
4. a
5. c
6. a
7. b
8. c
9. b
10. c

11. a
12. b
13. b
14. c
15. b
16. b
17. a
18. a
19. c
20. c

CHAPTER 5

Les professions et les carrières – Professions and careers

- *avoir les dents longues* – to be ambitious; to have one's sights set high

Literally: to have long teeth

Elle a les dents longues celle-là. Elle réussira dans la vie !

She's an ambitious one! She'll go far in life!

Originally, this expression used to mean simply 'to be hungry' (you can imagine the saliva dripping over the long fangs of the wolf). In the 19th century it took on the figurative meaning of being ambitious.

If somebody is really ambitious, you can exaggerate the expression and say, *"Il a les dents qui rayent le parquet"* (literally he has teeth which scratch the wooden floor).

- ***chacun son métier, les vaches seront bien gardées (proverbe)*** – you should stick to what you know and not meddle with things you don't understand; you do your job and I'll do mine

Literally: each his trade, the cows will be well looked after

Si vous aviez embauché un vrai comptable au lieu de faire vos comptes vous-même, vous n'auriez pas eu tous ces ennuis avec les impôts. Chacun son métier, les vaches seront bien gardées.

If you had employed a real accountant instead of doing your accounts yourself, you wouldn't have had all these problems with the taxes. You should stick to what you know and not meddle with what you don't understand.

This saying comes from a fable by Florian (1755-1794) called "*Le vacher et le garde-chasse*", 'the cowherd and the gamekeeper' (in fact, some say it goes right back to Aristotle). In this poem the gamekeeper is tired out after chasing a roe-deer all day long without success. Colin, who is bored with watching his father's cows, offers to hunt down the deer himself and leaves the gamekeeper to watch the cows in his place. He takes the gamekeeper's dog and his gun, sees the deer, misses his shot and hurts the poor dog instead. When he returns to the meadow, he finds the gamekeeper asleep and all the cows have been stolen. On hearing the news, Colin's father is furious and beats him with a stick saying: "*chacun son métier, / les vaches seront bien gardées*". A quick search on the internet will find you the fable. It's short and easy to read.

When this expression is used in its entirety, there is always a note of aggression or reproach in it. However, if you just say, "*Chacun son métier, hein !*" it can be quite gentle.

- ***il n'y a pas de sot métier, il n'y a que de sottes gens* (*proverbe*)** – every trade has its value

Literally: there are no stupid jobs, there are only stupid people

« *Il est ouvrier.*

– *Il n'y a pas de sot métier !* »

"He's a factory worker."

"Well, there's nothing wrong with that!"

- ***monter sur les planches*** – to go on the stage; to tread the boards

Literally: to get up on the planks

J'ai l'intention de m'inscrire à une troupe de théâtre et je vais gagner ma vie à monter sur les planches.

I intend joining a theatre group and I am going to earn my living treading the boards.

ⓘ

If an actor gives a spirited performance, you could also say, "*Il* ou *elle brûle les planches*" (literally he *or* she burns the planks).

- *vivre de sa plume* – to live by one's pen

Literally: to live by one's quill pen

Beaucoup d'auteurs publiés ont un autre métier parce qu'il est très difficile de vivre de sa plume.

Many published authors have another job because it is very difficult to live by one's pen.

Aller bien – going well

- *ça fait marcher les affaires* – it's good for business

Literally: that makes the business work

Pour les journaux un mariage de célébrités, ça fait marcher les affaires.

For newspapers a celebrity wedding is good for business.

- *c'est une véritable* ou *vraie ruche* – It's a hive of activity

Literally: it is a true *or* real (bee) hive

Quand je suis arrivé au centre opérationnel à Paris, tout le monde était très affairé et il y avait un va-et-vient incessant de personnel et de clients. Tout le monde s'activait. C'était une véritable ruche !

When I arrived at the operational centre in Paris, everyone was very busy and there was a constant coming and going of staff and clients. Everyone was bustling about. It was a hive of activity!

- *construire en dur* – to build a permanent structure

Literally: to build in hard

Les réfugiés vivent depuis six mois dans des tentes, mais nous allons construire en dur.

The refugees have been living in tents for six months, but we are going to build permanent structures.

- *être à l'honneur* – to have pride of place; to be much in evidence

Literally: to be at the honour

Nos nouveaux produits seront à l'honneur à la foire.

Our new products will have pride of place at the trade fair.

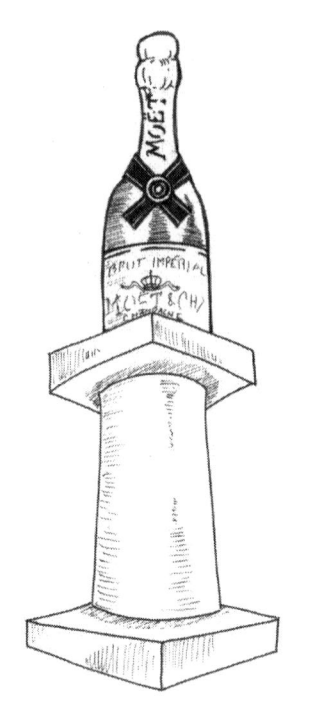

- *être au rendez-vous* – to be there; to show up

Literally: to be at the meeting

La foire aux antiquités a été couronnée de succès. Le soleil et la foule étaient au rendez-vous.

The antiques fair was a great success. There was sunshine and there were crowds.

- *faire boule de neige* – to snowball; to catch on quickly; to gather momentum

Literally: to make snowball

- *faire un effet boule de neige* – to have a ripple *or* snowball effect

Literally: to make a snowball effect

Cela démontre comment une idée ingénieuse peut faire boule de neige.

That shows how one clever idea can snowball.

- ***faire des affaires en or*** – to do a roaring trade

Literally: to do golden business

Cet hôtel est un bel établissement propre, confortable et très bien situé. Il a acquis une telle réputation que ses patrons font des affaires en or.

This is a beautiful hotel, clean, comfortable and very well situated. It has gained such a reputation, it is doing a roaring trade.

- *faire le plein* – to have a full house; to play to a full house

Literally: to make the full

Le spectacle a fait le plein tous les soirs. J'ai essayé d'avoir un billet, mais je n'ai pas pu.

The show played to a full house every night. I tried to get a ticket, but I couldn't.

You could also say, "*Le spectacle a joué **à guichets fermés**"* (literally with closed windows, referring to the box office which can be closed when all the tickets have been sold).

- *faire un malheur* – to be a big hit; to be all the rage

Literally: to make a misfortune

Ce film va faire un malheur.

This film is going to be a big hit.

Faire un malheur has two entirely opposite meanings. It has a positive meaning when used about a show or a film, for example, and then it also has an entirely negative meaning as in the following:

S'il continue à m'ennuyer, je fais un malheur* !

If he carries on annoying me, I'll do something I'll regret!

This negative use of *faire un malheur* has been around since the middle of the 19th century, with the positive meaning developing only quite recently.

A similar thing has happened to the expression *faire mal*: *ce film, il va faire mal*, 'this film is going to be a big hit' (literally this film, it's going to do harm).

- ***les petits ruisseaux font les grandes rivières (proverbe)*** – mighty oaks from little acorns grow (proverb)

Literally: little streams make big rivers

J'ai ouvert ma première petite boutique en 2005, puis deux autres en 2007 et, les petits ruisseaux faisant les grandes rivières, j'ai une chaîne de magasins maintenant.

I opened my first little shop in 2005, then two more in 2007 and, as mighty oaks from little acorns grow, I've now got a chain of stores.

This very popular proverb has been around since at least the 17th century.

- ***marcher du tonnerre (de Dieu)*** – to be going really well

Literally: to go of (God's) thunder

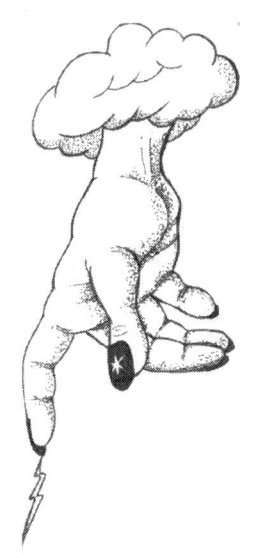

« *Comment marche votre salon de manucure ?*

– Ça marche du tonnerre ! »

"How is your nail bar business going?"

"It's going really well!"

ⓘ

Du tonnerre can be used as an adverb, as in the example above, or as an adjective: *nous avons passé des vacances du tonnerre,* 'we had a fantastic holiday'. Don't confuse *du tonnerre de Dieu* with the expression **Tonnerre de Dieu !** and the favourite expression of Captain Haddock of Tintin fame, **Tonnerre de Brest !** These are mild swearwords meaning something like 'Hell and damnation!'

- *mettre au point* – to perfect (technique); to bring into focus (camera); to develop (invention *or* medicine *or* system); to tune (motor); to finalize (project)

Literally: to put to the point

Nos chercheurs ont passé six ans à mettre au point ce médicament. Vous pouvez avoir confiance.

Our researchers have spent six years perfecting this medicine. You can have confidence.

- *réussir son coup* – to carry it off; to pull it off

Literally: to succeed one's blow

Pourra-t-il réussir son coup ? Ce sera très difficile, mais je crois qu'il réussira.

Will he be able to pull it off? It will be very difficult, but I think he'll succeed.

- *se vendre comme des petits pains* – to sell like hot cakes

Literally: to sell like small bread rolls

Les billets pour le prochain concert au Stade de France se vendent comme des petits pains.

Tickets for the next concert at the Stade de France are selling like hot cakes.

- *un jour à marquer d'une pierre blanche* – a very good day which is worth remembering for a long time; a momentous day; a milestone

Literally: a day to mark with a white stone

Après 10 ans d'absence, nos enfants sont rentrés hier d'Australie. Ce jour est à marquer d'une pierre blanche.

After 10 years of absence, our children came home from Australia yesterday. It was a momentous day for us.

Black and white have long been associated with bad and good. In classical times, the members of a jury placed in front of them either a black or a white pebble to signify a guilty or a not guilty verdict. In the same period, a white pebble engraved with a person's name was also used as an invitation to a banquet. It's not surprising then that a wonderful day to remember might be thought of as a day to mark on the calendar with a white pebble. The opposite is also true, and *un jour à marquer d'une pierre noire* also exists in French.

Quiz 5

1. « *Est-ce qu'il a plu sur la foire hier ?*
– *Non, le soleil était …* »
a) *à la conférence.*
b) *au rendez-vous.*
c) *dans une réunion.*

2. *Avec ses ventes record, je crois qu'elle pourrait bien réussir … et devenir représentante de l'année.*
a) *son cou*
b) *son coup*
c) *ses coupes*

3. *Le restaurant était bondé et les serveurs couraient dans tous les sens. C'était une vraie …*
a) *bûche.*
b) *cruche.*
c) *ruche.*

4. *La plupart des comédiens ne sont pas bien payés. Notre fille ne va pas gagner sa vie à monter sur les …*
a) *planches.*
b) *tranches.*
c) *branches.*

5. *Les petits ruisseaux font …*
a) *les grands océans.*
b) *les grandes rivières.*
c) *les flaques d'eau.*

6. *Le spectacle était merveilleux et le théâtre a fait …*
a) *le plein.*
b) *la pleine.*
c) *la plaine.*

7. *Un jour il sera quelqu'un, car il a les dents…*
a) *longues.*
b) *acérées.*
c) *pointues.*

8. *Il a fallu cinq ans pour … cette technique.*
a) *passer au point*
b) *faire à point*
c) *mettre au point*

9. *« Que fait-il dans la vie ?*
– Il est balayeur.
– Il n'y a pas de … métier ! »
a) *beau*
b) *sot*
c) *faux*

10. *Les fleuristes aiment le 14 février. Pour eux la Saint-Valentin fait … les affaires.*
a) *manger*
b) *marcher*
c) *marché*

11. *Je vais écrire un roman et essayer de vivre de …*
a) *mon encre.*
b) *mon crayon.*
c) *ma plume.*

12. *Nous allons détruire les bâtiments préfabriqués et construire en …*
a) *dur.*
b) *cuir.*
c) *carton.*

13. *L'idée a fait boule de …*
a) *neige.*
b) *glace.*
c) *cristal.*

14. *Les produits agricoles de la région seront … à la foire.*
a) *honnêtes*
b) *à l'hommage*
c) *à l'honneur*

15. *Tout va bien pour son entreprise. Il fait des affaires en …*
a) *argent.*
b) *or.*
c) *plomb.*

16. *J'adore ce film ! Je suis sûr qu'il va faire …*
a) *un mal content.*
b) *un malheureux.*
c) *un malheur.*

17. *Tout va bien pour sa nouvelle boulangerie. Ça marche …*
a) *de tonnerre.*
b) *d'éclair.*
c) *du tonnerre.*

18. *Tout le monde veut le nouveau smartphone. Ils se vendent comme …*
a) *des petits pains.*
b) *des baguettes chaudes.*
c) *des gâteaux chauds.*

19. *Hier notre chiffre d'affaires a battu tous les records. C'était un jour à marquer d'une pierre …*
a) *noire.*
b) *grise.*
c) *blanche.*

20. *Pour réaliser les installations électriques, il faut un électricien installateur. N'essayez pas de les faire vous-même. Chacun son métier, les ... seront bien gardées.*
a) *brebis*
b) *poules*
c) *vaches*

Answers 5

1.	b	11.	c
2.	b	12.	a
3.	c	13.	a
4.	a	14.	c
5.	b	15.	b
6.	a	16.	c
7.	a	17.	c
8.	c	18.	a
9.	b	19.	c
10.	b	20.	c

CHAPTER 6

L'aide et les dettes – help and indebtedness

- ***c'est donnant donnant*** – it's give and take

Literally: it is giving giving

C'est donnant donnant. Il m'aide avec mes déclarations de revenus et je lui donne des cours particuliers d'anglais.

It's give and take. He helps me with my tax returns and I give him private English lessons.

- ***donner un coup de main à quelqu'un*** – to lend somebody a hand

Literally: to give a blow of hand to somebody

Donnez-moi un coup de main, s'il vous plaît. Je ne peux pas porter cette machine tout seul.

Give me a hand, please. I can't carry this machine on my own.

- ***donner un coup de pouce*** – to give a nudge in the right direction; to help something along

Literally: to give a blow of thumb

Je ne savais pas quel logiciel choisir, mais Michel m'a donné un coup de pouce.

I didn't know which software program to choose, but Michel gave me a nudge in the right direction.

- ***être pistonné**** – to have friends who have pulled strings*

Literally: to be "pistonned"

- ***obtenir un poste par piston**** – to get a job through string-pulling*

Literally: to get a job through piston

- ***se faire pistonner**** – to have strings pulled for you*

Literally: to get oneself "pistonned"

Dans notre entreprise, la sélection se fait en considérant soit les compétences, soit à la fois les diplômes et la personnalité ; jamais par piston !

In our firm, appointments are made based upon ability or upon a mixture of qualifications and personality; never by string-pulling!

(i)

Probably the most notorious attempted use of the *piston* in France in recent memory was that of Jean Sarkozy. In 2009, the son of the then president, Nicolas Sarkozy, had his name

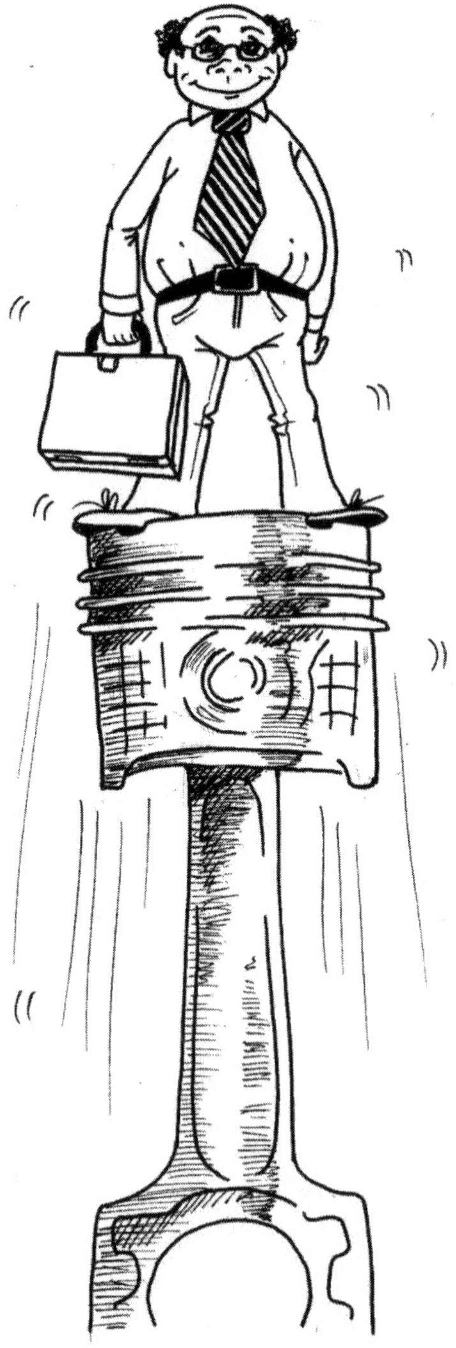

put forward for a very high status position as head of *Epad*, the development agency for *La Défense*, the business district in Paris. It was a post for which the young man was extremely lacking in qualifications. After an enormous public outcry at such blatant nepotism, Jean Sarkozy reluctantly withdrew his candidature. Do an internet search on "*Jean Sarkozy fiston piston*" and see what comes up!

- *faire corps* – to form one body; to be joined

Literally: to make body

Montrant une surprenante unanimité, les syndicats font corps, face aux propositions du gouvernement.

Surprisingly unanimous, the unions are joining together, faced with government proposals.

(i)

The English language has borrowed from the French the expression *esprit de corps*, meaning 'a shared spirit of comradeship, enthusiasm, and devotion to a cause among the members of a group, for example of a military unit'.

- *faire la courte échelle à quelqu'un* – to give somebody a leg up *or* a boost; to help somebody overcome an obstacle

Literally: to make somebody the short ladder

J'ai travaillé sur son CV, fait un bilan professionnel, lui ai donné des conseils et des informations : bref, je lui ai fait la courte échelle.

I worked on her CV, gave her a professional appraisal, gave her advice and information: in short, I gave her a leg up.

(i)

Have you ever needed to scale a wall or a fence but you just can't find enough hand and foot holes to clamber over the obstacle? What you need is for some kind person to clasp their hands together and make a step for you to climb upon (called "a pog up" in the North West of England). It's like providing a short ladder, *une courte échelle*, to give them that extra height. The expression is used figuratively when you give someone a boost to help them up the career ladder.

- ***j'ai besoin de vos lumières*** – I need the benefit of your wisdom *or* knowledge

Literally: I have need of your lights

J'ai besoin de vos lumières, madame. Pouvez-vous me montrer comment ouvrir ce fichier joint ?

I need the benefit of your wisdom, please. Can you show me how to open this attachment?

- ***je vous dois une fière chandelle*** – I am terribly indebted to you

Literally: I owe you a proud candle

Je vous remercie de votre aide. Je vous dois une fière chandelle.

Thank you for your help. I'm terribly indebted to you.

Once we realize that *fier / fière* once meant large or important, this expression is easier to understand. In times past, when someone did some great service for you, you would go straight to church and light a large candle for them in order to show your gratitude. According to Alain Rey in his *Le Dictionnaire historique de la langue française*, this expression goes right back to the middle of the 17th century.

- ***mettre la main à la pâte*** – to lend a hand; to muck in

Literally: to put the hand to the dough

Il y a beaucoup à faire et tout le monde, sans exception, doit mettre la main à la pâte.

There's a lot to do and everyone, without exception, must lend a hand.

- ***prêter main-forte à quelqu'un*** – to come to somebody's assistance

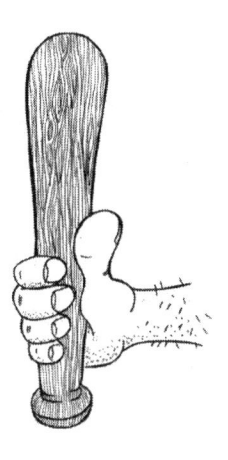

Literally: to lend somebody strong-hand

La gestion des traductions est assez lourde, mais on s'en sortira grâce à Virginie qui va nous prêter main-forte dans ce domaine.

Managing the translations is rather a heavy task, but we will get through it thanks to Virginie who is going to come to our assistance in this area.

Back in the 15th century, law enforcers sometimes needed help from ordinary folk to maintain law and order and this is where this expression comes from. Later, the meaning generalized to mean 'lending a hand' in any context.

- *renvoyer l'ascenseur* – to return the favour

Literally: to send back the lift

Je lui ai fait une faveur l'année dernière ; donc, je suis sûr qu'elle me renverra l'ascenseur.

I did her a favour last year, so I'm sure she will return the favour.

- ***se mettre en quatre pour aider quelqu'un* ou *pour faire quelque chose*** – to bend over backwards to help somebody *or* to do something

Literally: to split oneself into four to help somebody *or* to do something

Nous avons pensé qu'on nous dirait que c'était impossible, mais le personnel s'est mis en quatre pour nous aider à réussir le coup.

We thought we'd be told it was impossible, but the workforce bent over backwards to help us pull it off.

- *se tenir* ou *se serrer les coudes* – to stick together

Literally: to hold each other's elbows *or* to squeeze together the elbows

Dans leur équipe, il règne un formidable esprit de solidarité. Donc, quand ça chauffe, ils se serrent les coudes.

There's a tremendous spirit of solidarity in their team, so when there's trouble, they stick together.

Le travail facile – easy work

- *c'est le B.A.-BA* ou *le b.a.-ba (de)* – it's the very basics (of); it's the ABC (of)

Literally: it is the B.A.-BA (of);

- *être au B.A.-BA* – to be a beginner

Literally: to be at the B.A.-BA

Ça ne sert à rien de demander à Joël. Il n'en est qu'au B.A.-BA.

There's no point in asking Joël. He's just a beginner.

The first two letters B and A are pronounced like the individual letters of the French alphabet and the BA is pronounced as one syllable.

One method of teaching children to read in France is the syllabic method where letters are put together to be read as one syllable; hence B.A. = BA (this is opposed to the global method where the whole word is recognized). So if someone is still learning basic skills, he or she is a real beginner and you wouldn't want to ask them to do a tricky job for you.

- *c'est l'enfance de l'art* – it's simple

Literally: it is the infancy of the art

Pour réparer une fuite d'eau, il faut simplement changer le joint de robinet. C'est peut-être l'enfance de l'art pour un plombier, mais pas pour moi !

To repair a leak, you just need to change the washer. It might be simple for a plumber, but not for me!

- *c'est un jeu d'enfant* – it's child's play

Literally: it is a child's game

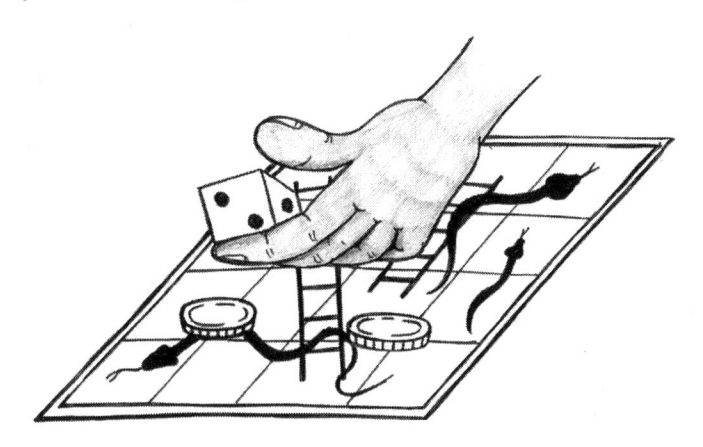

Télécharger une vidéo, c'est un jeu d'enfant. Suivez les instructions faciles ci-dessous.

Uploading a video is child's play. Follow these simple instructions below.

- *c'est simple comme bonjour** – it's a cinch**; it's as easy as ABC*; it's as easy as pie*

Literally: it is as easy as hello

Voulez-vous savoir comment sauvegarder un fichier ? Eh bien, c'est simple comme bonjour !

Do you want to know how to save a file? Well, it's as easy as pie!

- ***faire d'une pierre deux coups (proverbe)*** – to kill two birds with one stone (proverb)

Literally: to make two blows with one stone

Ils ont fait d'une pierre deux coups : en rentrant de la conférence à Marseille, ils ont visité leur succursale à Avignon.

They killed two birds with one stone: coming back from the conference in Marseille, they visited their branch in Avignon.

Montaigne used this expression right back in the 16th century. It is a metaphor easy to understand. If you were out with a catapult and you managed to hit two of whatever you were aiming at with just one stone, you would be rather pleased with yourself. It means 'to complete two actions with the effort normally needed for just one'.

- *faire quelque chose au pifomètre**; calculer au pifomètre*** – to do something by guesswork; to do a guesstimate*

Literally: to do something by the "noseometer"

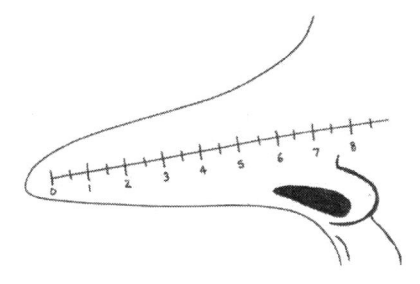

On ne peut pas concevoir un gratte-ciel au pifomètre.

You can't design a sky-scraper using guesswork.

Le pif is the slang word for the nose and relates to intuition. Of course, this lovely word *pifomètre* has been invented because it sounds like the more serious measuring instrument, *le baromètre*. If you assess something only by what your nose or intuition tells you, you are using your *pifomètre*.

- *manger son pain blanc en premier* – to have it easy at the start; to start with the best and leave the worst till later

Literally: to eat one's white bread first

Pour son premier jour dans son nouveau boulot, on lui a donné quelques petites tâches faciles à faire et il a été bien content, mais il va s'apercevoir qu'il a mangé son pain blanc en premier. Demain le vrai travail commencera !

For his first day in his new job, he was given a few easy tasks to do and he was happy, but he's soon going to realize that he's just had it easy to start with. Tomorrow the real work begins!

Let's think back to the 16th century when this expression is first noted. At that time, most people ate loaves of a greyish colour, *le pain noir*, and only the rich used refined white flour for their daily bread. When the peasants did have the chance to buy white flour, which they considered to be of superior quality and flavour, they would have been more inclined to eat that first and to keep the courser bread for later. You can use this expression in any situation now, where the more pleasant or easier task is happily done first, but a less agreeable experience awaits.

Quiz 6

1. Je ne sais pas exactement combien il nous en faudra. J'ai fait le calcul au ...
a) *pifomètre.*
b) *nezomètre.*
c) *baromètre.*

2. Je peux vous aider, mais il faut me renvoyer ... après.
a) *l'escalier roulant*
b) *l'échelle*
c) *l'ascenseur*

3. Ce que je t'apprends, c'est vraiment le ... de l'architecture.
a) *B.A.-BA*
b) *baba*
c) *BA –BA*

4. Elle avance rapidement toute seule sans demander rien à personne. On n'a pas besoin de lui faire la courte ...
a) *échelle.*
b) *échine.*
c) *écharpe.*

5. *Les Européens font … pour défendre l'euro.*
a) *cœur*
b) *corne*
c) *corps*

6. *Mme Lambert s'est mise en … pour nous aider à trouver un logement près du chantier.*
a) *quatre*
b) *trois*
c) *sept*

7. *Si vous avez besoin d'aide ce soir, je peux vous donner …*
a) *une coupe de main.*
b) *un cul de main.*
c) *un coup de main.*

8. *Il faut simplement le dévisser. C'est … de l'art.*
a) *l'enfant*
b) *l'enfance*
c) *l'enfantement*

9. *Le travail a été monstrueux et nous devons surtout remercier Francis qui nous a prêté…*
a) *pied-fort.*
b) *bras-fort.*
c) *main-forte.*

10. *Il y a trop à faire pour une personne, donc je vais mettre la main …*
a) *au pâté.*
b) *à la pâte.*
c) *à la pâtée.*

11. *Il mange gratuitement dans mon restaurant parce qu'il m'aide avec mes comptes. C'est …*
a) *donner donner.*
b) *donner donnant.*
c) *donnant donnant.*

12. *Mon nouveau supérieur direct est le fils du patron. Il s'est fait … bien sûr !*
a) *pitonner.*
b) *apitoyer.*
c) *pistonner.*

13. *Elle ne sait pas où commencer avec son projet. Je vais lui donner un petit coup …*
a) *de doigt.*
b) *de pouce.*
c) *d'orteil.*

14. *S'il vous plaît, M. Faure, je ne comprends pas ce logiciel et j'ai besoin de vos …*
a) *luminaires.*
b) *lumières.*
c) *lanternes.*

15. *Merci beaucoup, Mme Dupont. Je vous dois …*
a) *une fière bougie.*
b) *une grande chandelle.*
c) *une fière chandelle.*

16. *C'est aussi simple que ça. C'est … d'enfant.*
a) *un jouet*
b) *un nounours*
c) *un jeu*

17. *Si vous venez avec moi demain, on peut faire …*
a) *de deux pierres un coup.*
b) *d'une pierre deux coups.*
c) *d'un coup deux pierres.*

18. *Pour se battre contre cette injustice, il faut se serrer les …*
a) *cous.*
b) *coudes.*
c) *culs.*

19. *Avec ce manuel facile, c'est simple comme …*
a) *salut.*
b) *bonsoir.*
c) *bonjour.*

20. *Ayant décidé de refaire la décoration de ma maison, j'ai commencé avec la salle à manger. J'ai mangé ... le premier, car le reste de la maison a été beaucoup plus difficile à faire.*
a) *mon pain blanc*
b) *ma baguette*
c) *mon pain noir*

Answers 6

1. a
2. c
3. a
4. a
5. c
6. a
7. c
8. b
9. c
10. b
11. c
12. c
13. b
14. b
15. c
16. c
17. b
18. b
19. c
20. a

CHAPTER 7

Les heures de travail et les habitudes – Working hours and habits

- *bosser au black** – see *travailler au noir*

- *faire le pont* – to take an extra day off work to make a long week-end of it

Literally: to make the bridge

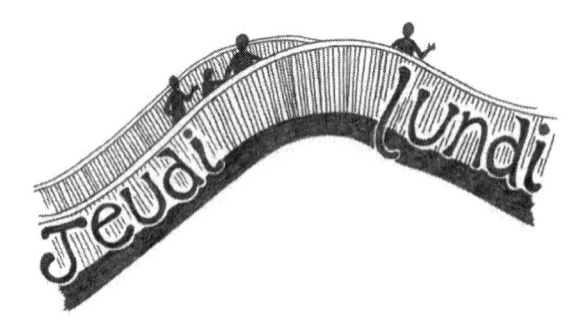

Cette année, l'Assomption est un mardi, donc je vais faire le pont.

This year, Assumption Day is on a Tuesday, so I'm going to take the Monday off to make a long week-end of it.

ⓘ

Apart from Easter Monday, *le lundi de Pâques,* Whit Monday, *le lundi de Pentecôte,* and Ascension Day, *le jeudi de l'Ascension,*

French public holidays, *les jours fériés*, are fixed by date, not by the day of the week. If a public holiday, such as *la fête du Travail* on May 1st, falls on a Thursday or a Tuesday, then many workers also take off the Friday or Monday (*ils font le pont*). Often, businesses close for the whole four days. Practices vary: some workers are given an extra day's holiday but others have to use a day of their annual leave or make up for hours lost by working extra hours at another time.

- *faire les trois-huit* ; *faire les 3 x 8* – to operate round the clock working in eight-hour shifts

Literally: to make the three-eight

Dans notre usine, on fait les trois-huit. Cette semaine, je suis d'équipe de nuit.

In our factory, we work shifts. This week, I'm working nights.

- ***prendre le pli de faire quelque chose*** – to get into the habit of doing something

Literally: to take the fold *or* crease of doing something

J'ai pris le pli de lire mes e-mails en buvant mon premier café de la journée.

I have got into the habit of reading my emails whilst drinking my first coffee of the day.

If you have a smart crease down the front and back of your trousers, it is easy to fold them and they hang nicely. It takes very little thought or effort to make the fabric fall back into the correct position. The crease we are dealing with in this expression is like a crease in your state of mind, which creates a habit. When something becomes a habit, it slots into your daily routine, just as well-tailored trousers fall naturally into place.

- ***travailler au noir ; bosser au black*** * – to work illegally; to moonlight

Literally: to work in the black

La victime de l'accident n'a pas voulu le signaler aux autorités parce qu'elle travaillait au noir sur le chantier.

The victim of the accident didn't want to report it to the authorities because he was working illegally on the worksite.

Are you thinking this expression might come from the slave trade? Well, you'd be wrong! It seems that this expression has nothing to do with the slave trade, but comes from medieval times, when it was illegal for an employer to make his employees work after daylight. Unscrupulous employers broke the law and made their workers work by candlelight; hence the expression *travailler au noir*.

Avoir de l'influence ou du pouvoir – having influence or power

- *avoir le bras long* – to be influential

Literally: to have the long arm

Ne vous inquiétez pas. Mon oncle a le bras long et il nous obtiendra le permis de construire nécessaire.

Don't worry. My uncle is influential and he will get us the necessary planning permission.

- ***être connu comme le loup blanc*** – to be known all over; to be very well known

Literally: to be known like the white wolf

Depuis que j'ai joué dans « Plus belle la vie », je suis connu comme le loup blanc.

Since I played in the TV series "*Plus belle la vie*", I'm known all over.

When wolves roamed France, villagers were constantly keeping an eye out for them, as they didn't want their sheep being snapped up for a tasty supper. Imagine if there had been an albino wolf in the neighbourhood. Word would soon have got round and everybody would be in the know and on the look-out for it.

- *être un requin (de la finance)* – to be a shark (of the financial world); to be ruthless, greedy and dishonest

Literally: to be a shark (of finance)

C'est un requin de la finance – il ne voit que l'aspect financier de ses opérations.

He's a shark of the financial world – he sees only the financial aspect of his operations.

- *être une grosse légume* ou une huile** – to be a bigwig* *or* a big-shot*

Literally: to be a large vegetable *or* an oil

Nous avons invité toutes les grosses légumes : le maire, le commissaire de police et les chefs d'industrie.

We have invited all the big-shots: the mayor, the chief of police and the heads of industry.

ⓘ

Légume is masculine in modern French, apart from in this colloquial expression, where it is feminine.

- ***faire la pluie et le beau temps*** – to be all powerful; to make all the decisions; to call all the shots

Literally: to make the rain and the fine weather

Quand il travaillait à son propre compte, il faisait la pluie et le beau temps, mais maintenant il doit faire ce que son supérieur hiérarchique lui dit de faire.

When he worked for himself, he called all the shots, but now he has to do what his line manager tells him to do.

- *mieux vaut avoir affaire au bon Dieu qu'à ses saints (proverbe)* – better to go straight to the top man

Literally: it is better to do business with the good God than with his saints

J'écris directement au président de la République. Mieux vaut avoir affaire au bon Dieu qu'à ses saints.

I'm writing directly to the President of the Republic. Better to go straight to the top man.

Une sale affaire – nasty business

- *accusé de jouer (un) double jeu* – accused of double-dealing

Literally: accused of playing (a) double game

Ils prétendent nous soutenir, mais dans le dos ils nous attaquent. Je les accuse de jouer un double jeu.

They claim to be supporting us, but they are attacking us behind our backs. I'm accusing them of double-dealing.

- ***casser du sucre sur le dos de quelqu'un*** * – to gossip *or* talk about somebody behind his *or* her back

Literally: to break sugar on somebody's back

Dès qu'elle sortait, ses collègues se mettaient à casser du sucre sur son dos.

As soon as she went out, her co-workers started to gossip about her behind her back.

The origin of this expression, first noted in 1868, is not clear. Sugar did come in large blocks which had to be broken up for sale but this doesn't get us very far, except that the violence of this act echoes the breaking of the reputation of the person being gossiped about. Also, *sucrer* was a slang word meaning 'to treat badly', so that might have some significance. *Sur le dos* is interesting because we might bear a weight or responsibility on our backs (or on our shoulders in English) so the person being talked about will have to bear the burden of what is being said about him or her. Duneton points out that, going back a further hundred years to the 18th century, *se sucrer de quelqu'un* meant 'to take somebody for an imbecile', so it may be that the meaning has slipped a little over time.

- *faire des affaires sur le dos de quelqu'un* – to do a bit of business at somebody's expense

Literally: to do business on somebody's back

Les grandes entreprises étrangères qui s'installent dans notre pays sans payer d'impôts font des affaires sur le dos du contribuable.

The large foreign companies who set up in our country without paying taxes are doing so at the taxpayer's expense.

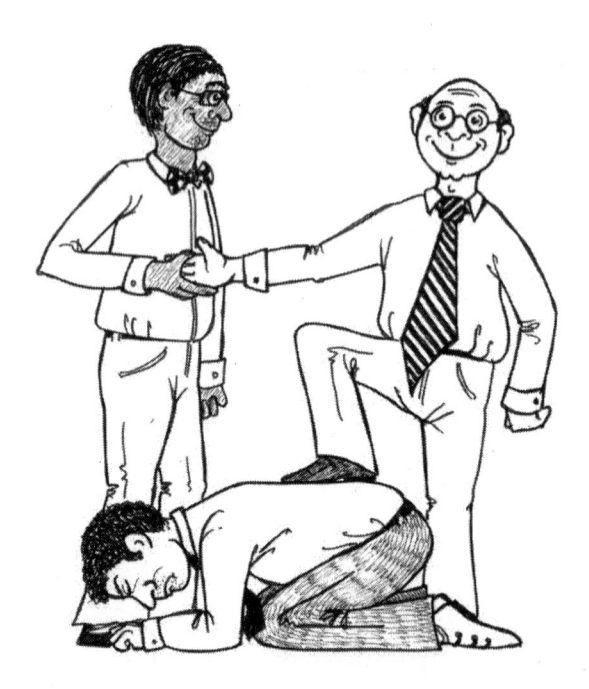

- *je ne mange pas de ce pain-là* – I'm having nothing to do with that; I'm not stooping to anything like that

Literally: I don't eat that bread

Je refuse d'être complice de cet acte scandaleux. Je ne mange pas de ce pain-là !

I refuse to be party to this disgraceful act. I want nothing to do with it!

The origins of this expression are not known but bread is often used as a metaphor for basic needs. Someone who is willing to go hungry, rather than stooping to dirty dealing, is an honest person. Less scrupulous people would be willing to do whatever it takes "to earn a crust".

- *la fin justifie les moyens (proverbe)* – the end justifies the means (proverb)

Literally: the end justifies the means

Il y a eu beaucoup de dégâts, mais après tout, la fin justifie les moyens, n'est-ce pas ?

There's been a lot of damage, but after all, the end justifies the means, doesn't it?

The origin of this proverb is disputed but it is often attributed to the Italian Nicolò Machiavelli (1469-1527), the founder of modern political science. He wrote a book called *The Prince* in which he seemed to be condoning the unscrupulous politicians' immoral behaviour. However, the exact words of the proverb are not to be found in *The Prince*.

Others say we have Philippe van den Clyte (1445-1509) to thank for this proverb. He was the Seigneur de Commynes, a French historian and scholar. He betrayed Charles the Bold (*Charles le Téméraire*) to enter the service of Louis XI, who made him rich and powerful.

- ***les affaires sont les affaires (proverbe)*** – business is business (proverb)

Literally: business is business

Beaucoup de gens vont souffrir quand on construira ce barrage, mais les affaires sont les affaires et il ne faut pas s'inquiéter des problèmes d'autrui.

Lots of people will suffer when this dam is built, but business is business and we mustn't worry about other people's problems.

The French borrowed this expression from the English proverb "business is business" which dates from the 18th century.

"*Les Affaires sont les affaires*" is the name of a comic stage play written by Octave Mirbeau in 1903, which is still a favourite of theatre-goers today. You can easily find clips of it on the internet. The play is about a rich businessman, Isidore Lechat, a man without scruples, who wants to enter parliament and marry off his unwilling daughter to a nobleman she detests. She decides to run off with a poor chemist instead, a choice which profoundly shocked the critics of the day. The stage play was made into a film in 1942 by Jean Dréville and into a TV film in 2012 starring Christian Clavier and Régis Laspalès.

- ***prendre des vessies pour des lanternes*** – to be fooled *or* badly mistaken

Literally: to take bladders for lanterns

Faites attention ! Elle veut nous faire prendre des vessies pour des lanternes, mais nous ne sommes pas dupes.

Be careful! She's trying to pull the wool over our eyes, but she doesn't fool us.

This idiom is a modern version of a much older expression, *vendre vessie pour lanterne*, 'to sell a bladder for a lantern'. Many years ago, pigs' bladders were inflated and dried out to use as containers. If a candle was placed inside them, they could be used as a lantern in an emergency, as the light could shine through them. You could try to trick someone by selling them a bladder as a beautiful lantern; hence the old expression which has since evolved a little into ***prendre des vessies pour des lanternes***.

- ***rouler quelqu'un dans la farine**** – to pull the wool over somebody's eyes; to deceive *or* dupe somebody

Literally: to roll somebody in flour

- ***se faire rouler dans la farine**** – to be deceived *or* duped; to be had*; to have the wool pulled over one's eyes

Literally: to have oneself rolled in flour

Je n'ai pas lu le contrat soigneusement et, par conséquent, je me suis fait rouler dans la farine.

I didn't read the contract carefully and, consequently, I was duped.

This 19th century expression is a happy combination of two ideas, each to do with being conned. ***Se faire rouler**** on its own means 'to be done'*: ***je me suis fait rouler !**** – I've been done!* *La farine* once had the meaning of 'deceitful arguments' and, also, might have referred to the makeup used by actors to disguise their faces when taking on a role. Put the two halves together and you have been well and truly duped!

(i)

When Jacques Chirac was *président de la République*, it was sometimes cheekily said that his Prime Minister (2002-2005) Jean-Pierre Raffarin *"roulait la population dans la raffarine"*.

- ***tailler un costard*** **ou** *une veste à quelqu'un** – to say nasty things about somebody; to run somebody down behind his *or* her back*; to criticize somebody severely

Literally: to cut out a suit *or* a jacket for somebody

Il n'a pas été épargné par la presse : partout on lui taille un costard.

He hasn't been spared by the press: everywhere nasty things are being said about him.

Un costard is a slang word for a suit or *un costume*. In the world of theatre, ***faire un costard*** or ***un costume*** was an old expression meaning 'to applaud an actor, even before he spoke'. Sometimes expressions completely reverse in meaning over time and this seems to have happened here, as ***tailler un costard*** means 'to say something nasty about someone'. It probably got mixed up with an older expression, ***habiller quelqu'un pour l'hiver*** (literally to dress somebody for the winter) which meant the same thing. There is the common idea of putting a garment on someone's back and figuratively burdening them. You can use this expression for saying something nasty to somebody's face or behind their back.

- *verser un pot-de-vin à quelqu'un* – to bribe somebody

Literally: to pour somebody a jug-of-wine

Il a versé un pot-de-vin au juge pour qu'il rende son jugement en sa faveur.

He bribed the judge so that he would rule in his favour.

Though this is not really a French expression, it is worth including. The idea of offering someone a drink to say thank you has been with us since time began but at some point in history the *pot-de-vin* started to mean not just a drink but money. It was first noted being used in the figurative sense in 1483. Then it simply meant 'money given as a tip for good service'. A century later it was being used to mean that money was being offered secretly in order to corrupt someone.

Quiz 7

1. *Je ne veux pas casser ... sur le dos du patron, mais je le trouve parfois un peu paresseux.*
a) *des œufs*
b) *du sucre*
c) *du sel*

2. *J'ai pris rendez-vous avec le PDG. Mieux vaut avoir affaire au bon Dieu qu'à ses ...*
a) *diables.*
b) *prêtres.*
c) *saints.*

3. *Il est sans scrupules. C'est ... de la finance.*
a) *un requin*
b) *une méduse*
c) *une pieuvre*

4. *Désolé, je regrette, mais...*
a) *l'affaire est l'affaire.*
b) *une affaire est une affaire.*
c) *les affaires sont les affaires.*

5. *Les sans-papiers travaillent au …*
a) *blanc.*
b) *noir.*
c) *rouge.*

6. *Cette année, la Toussaint est un mardi. Allez-vous faire … ?*
a) *le point*
b) *le poireau*
c) *le pont*

7. *Pour qu'il ne révèle pas son secret, on lui a versé …*
a) *une bouteille-de-vin.*
b) *une carafe-de-vin.*
c) *un pot-de-vin.*

8. *J'ai pris … de fumer une cigarette avant de commencer mon travail.*
a) *le mauvais prix*
b) *la mauvaise pluie*
c) *le mauvais pli*

9. *L'usine fonctionne vingt-quatre heures sur vingt-quatre et on fait les …*
a) *trois-huit.*
b) *huit-trois.*
c) *six-trois.*

10. *Mon beau-père nous aidera. Il a …*
a) *un long bras.*
b) *le long bras.*
c) *le bras long.*

11. *Il y a des businessmen sans scrupules qui font des affaires sur … des pauvres victimes.*
a) *la tête*
b) *les épaules*
c) *le dos*

12. *Le pauvre type s'est fait rouler dans … par un vendeur malhonnête.*
a) *le sucre*
b) *le sable*
c) *la farine*

13. *Tiens ! Tu ne le connais pas ? Mais il est connu comme …*
a) *le renard bleu.*
b) *le loup blanc.*
c) *le tigre tacheté.*

14. *J'ai un rendez-vous important ce matin avec les …*
a) *grosses légumes.*
b) *gros choux.*
c) *gros poireaux.*

15. *Quand il avait sa propre usine, il faisait ... et le beau temps.*
a) *les orages*
b) *la pluie*
c) *la neige*

16. *Il est hypocrite. Il sert les deux parties à la fois. Il joue ... jeu.*
a) *double*
b) *triple*
c) *doublé*

17. *C'est franchement honteux, mais ... justifie les moyens, n'est-ce pas ?*
a) *la faim*
b) *la fin*
c) *la feinte*

18. *Je n'aime pas dire du mal de lui pendant qu'il n'est pas là. Je ne vais pas lui tailler ...*
a) *un smoking.*
b) *un gilet.*
c) *une veste.*

19. *Même si d'autres le font, moi je ne mange pas ... ! C'est malhonnête !*
a) *de ce pain-là*
b) *de pain*
c) *de ce gâteau-là*

20. *Tu veux me faire prendre ... pour des lanternes ?*
a) *des ballons*
b) *des boyaux*
c) *des vessies*

Answers 7

1. b
2. c
3. a
4. c
5. b
6. c
7. c
8. c
9. a
10. c

11. c
12. c
13. b
14. a
15. b
16. a
17. b
18. c
19. a
20. c

CHAPTER 8

Avoir du mal - struggling

- *battre de l'aile* – to be in a bad way

Literally: to beat of the wing

Son salon de coiffure bat de l'aile faute de clients.

Her hairdressing salon is in a bad way through lack of customers.

This expression was first noted in 1611. If a bird is injured and is struggling to fly, it beats its wings desperately. The poor thing is destined to die, just like a business which is failing despite its last feeble attempts to stay afloat.

- *être dans ses petits souliers* – to be like a fish out of water; to feel pretty uncomfortable

Literally: to be in one's little shoes

Je devais aller le chercher à la gare, mais j'ai oublié. J'étais dans mes petits souliers quand je l'ai vu arriver en taxi.

I was supposed to pick him up from the station, but I forgot. I felt pretty uncomfortable when I saw him arriving by taxi.

Chaussure is used more often for shoe in modern French than *soulier*. This expression seems to be nonsensical until you know that an earlier version existed which was *être mal dans ses petits souliers* (to feel ill in one's little shoes). From feeling ill, it changed its meaning to being ill at ease then finally, by 1830, the *mal* was dropped leaving only *être dans ses petits souliers*. Imagine wearing not just small shoes but shoes which are so small they make you feel really uncomfortable.

- *je nage complètement** – I'm all at sea*; I'm completely lost

Literally: I am swimming completely

Pouvez-vous m'expliquer ce programme ? Je nage complètement.

Can you explain this schedule to me? I'm all at sea.

(i)

You can also use the verb *patauger** here, literally 'to wade about, to paddle or to splash about'. In a figurative sense it means 'to get bogged down' or 'to flounder'. Imagine someone wading through mud.

(Savoir) nager*, '(to know how) to swim', can be used colloquially to mean 'to manage' or 'to get by', possibly by using unscrupulous methods.

- *pédaler dans la choucroute*** – to be all at sea*; to be struggling and getting nowhere

    Literally: to be pedalling in sauerkraut

« Daniel semble se démener, mais il n'avance pas.

– Oui, je crois qu'il pédale dans la choucroute depuis son arrivée. »

"Daniel seems to be trying hard but getting nowhere."

"Yes, I think he's been all at sea since he got here."

The traditional method of making sauerkraut involved pressing the cabbage and this could have been done with the feet in the same way that grapes might be pressed; hence *pédaler*. You could do a lot of legwork without actually moving forward. Later variations on the saying extend the idea of foot movement to hand movement. They are ***pédaler dans la semoule***, 'semolina', ***le yaourt***, 'yoghurt', ***la purée***, 'purée' or ***le couscous***, 'couscous', all of which involve a lot of mixing with the hands (or, these days, a machine). ***Pédaler dans la choucroute*** and ***pédaler dans la semoule*** are the more common expressions.

- ***perdre pied*** – to be *or* to get out of one's depth; to lose one's footing

Literally: to lose foot

Quand j'ai commencé mon nouveau travail, il y avait tellement de choses à apprendre en si peu de temps que j'avais peur de perdre pied.

When I started my new job, there was so much to learn in so little time that I was afraid of getting out of my depth.

- *se noyer dans un verre d'eau* – to make heavy weather of the simplest of things

Literally: to drown in a glass of water

Dès qu'il rencontre la moindre petite difficulté, il se laisse dépasser. Il se noie dans un verre d'eau !

As soon as he meets the slightest difficulty, it's beyond him! He makes hard weather of the simplest of things!

In the 17th century the image was even more exaggerated as the expression used to be *se noyer dans un crachat* (to drown in spit) or *se noyer dans une goutte d'eau* (to drown in a drop of water).

Céder – giving in

- ***baisser les bras*** – to give in; to throw in the towel

Literally: to lower the arms

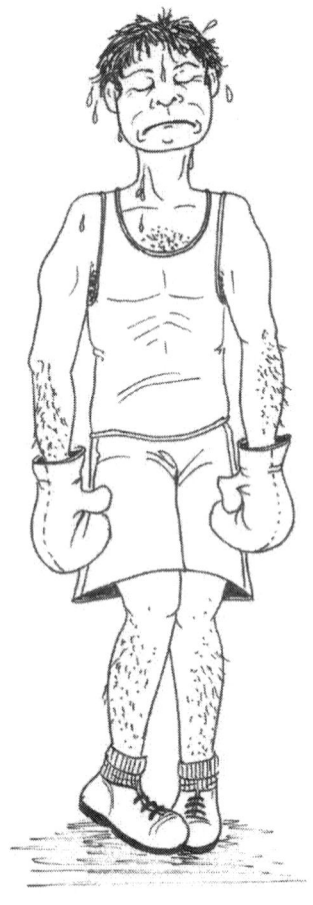

Ne baissez pas les bras. C'est difficile, mais nous nous débrouillerons.

Don't give in. It's difficult, but we will manage.

This expression may have come from the boxing ring. If you lower your gloves, you are giving your opponent the chance to make that winning blow which finishes you off and loses you the match.

An alternative explanation takes us back much further to Trial by Ordeal where it was necessary for a judge to come down upon the side of the one who was favoured by God. There might have been, for example, two men both claiming they had the right to own the same piece of land. One of the less horrible trials inflicted on claimants was for them to hold out their arms horizontally and whoever dropped them first was the loser. This was a method prized by Charlemagne (742?-814), the ruler of the Carolingian Empire.

- *jeter l'éponge* – to throw in the towel

Literally: to throw in the sponge

Après avoir subi des pertes s'élevant à 2 millions d'euros, je dois jeter l'éponge.

After having made a loss amounting to 2 million euros, I have to throw in the towel.

In English there used to be the same expression as in the French, "to throw in the sponge", but the sponge has now largely been replaced by a towel. It is another expression which comes from the world of boxing. If a boxer does not wish to continue a bout and wants to admit defeat, his trainer can throw in a sponge from their corner.

- *la goutte d'eau qui fait déborder le vase* – the last straw; the straw that breaks the camel's back

Literally: the drop of water that makes the vase overflow

« *J'ai seulement demandé à Aurélie qu'elle travaille une heure de plus cet après-midi et elle a fondu en larmes !*

– Ah, ça a été la goutte d'eau qui a fait déborder le vase. »

"I only asked Aurélie to work an extra hour this afternoon and she burst into tears."

"Ah, that was the last straw for her."

(i)

Did you know that the French word *vase* also exists in the feminine? *La vase* is the silt or mud you find at the bottom of a river but has nothing whatsoever to do with the flow of water in this expression.

L'échec – failure

- ***aller** ou **foncer droit dans le mur*** –to do something which can only lead to failure; to be heading for disaster

Literally: to go *or* tear straight into the wall

Le président a pris de très mauvaises décisions et maintenant le gouvernement conduit notre pays droit dans le mur.

The president has made very bad decisions and now the government is leading our country into disaster.

The origin of this expression is not clear, though it may well be related to the early days of motor racing. When a driver lost control of his vehicle, he would career off the course and end up hitting a wall and that would be that.

- ***aller* ou *s'en aller à vau-l'eau* ou *à la dérive*** – to go to the dogs*; to be in a state of collapse; to be on the road to ruin

Literally: to go *or* to go off to valley-the-water *or* with the current; to let things go drifting

Petit à petit, le marché de l'automobile s'en va à vau-l'eau dans notre pays.

Little by little, the motor industry is going to the dogs in our country.

This expression has nothing to do with baby cows (*veaux*). It has nothing to do with the verb *valoir* either. *Vau* is in fact an Old French word for a valley and it also meant 'downstream'. *Aller à vau* had the concrete meaning of 'to follow the flow of the water' until at least the middle of the 16th century. At this point it started to take on its figurative meaning and was used to refer to an enterprise which was doing very badly.

- ***c'est la fin des haricots**** – it's the end of the line; it's a complete disaster; there's no more hope

Literally: it is the end of the beans

« *Alors, c'est la fin des haricots ?*

– Oui, il n'y a plus d'espoir. »

"So, is it the end of the line?"

"Yes, there's no more hope."

At the beginning of the 20th century when this expression first appeared, board games and card games were very popular. If it was a betting game, rather than using real coins, sometimes dried beans were used as counters and when a player lost all his beans, the game came to an end.

That's one possible origin for this expression. Another is that in boarding schools or prisons, the humble bean was the cheapest way of filling hungry bellies and they were cooked when funds in the coffers were low. If there were no beans left, then it really was a hopeless situation.

- *courir à l'échec* – to be heading for failure

Literally: to run to the failure

Il est entré sur un marché en déclin et surpeuplé. Cela n'a rien d'étonnant s'il court à l'échec.

He has entered an overcrowded market in decline. It's not surprising if he's heading for failure.

- ***être au bout du rouleau*** – to be exhausted; to have come to the end of the road; to have run out of ideas; to be running short (of money)

Literally: to be at the end of the roll

Je suis au bout du rouleau. Je travaille dix-huit heures par jour et je n'en peux plus.

I've come to the end of the road. I work eighteen hours a day and I can't cope any more.

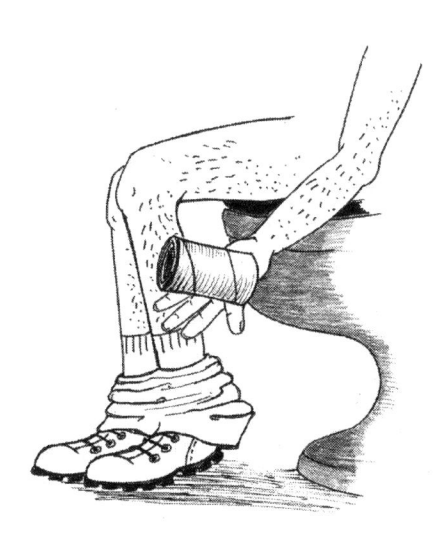

Back in ancient times, books were written on scrolls or *rouleaux* wound onto an ivory stick (you'll no doubt have seen them on statues of important Ancient Romans). These types of scrolls were used right up until the end of the 18th century for administrative purposes. The early French word for a scroll was *un role* or *un roole*. This same word was also used to mean 'the words one needed to recite in a stage play' and *un rollet* was 'a small theatre role'. By the end of the 17th century we had the expression **être au bout de son rollet**. If someone had run out of ideas in a discussion and didn't know what else to say, or had run out of ideas in any task they had begun, that person was **au bout de son rollet**.

The modern meaning has changed a little though. During the 18th century the meaning slid more towards running out of money rather than ideas. Coins in banks came wrapped in paper in a long roll or *rouleau*. So figuratively, if you were at the bottom of the roll of money, then you were broke. The Larousse in 1898 kept both meanings in its explanation: "*avoir épuisé tous ses arguments, tous ses moyens*", 'to have exhausted all of one's arguments or one's means'.

However, in modern French the expression **être au bout du rouleau** also means 'to be exhausted'. This, it seems, is because of the arrival on the scene of an important machine invented by Edison in 1877: the phonograph. The phonograph used indentations in a roll of tinfoil or wax to produce sound, and when the spring in the mechanism had largely uncoiled, the sound produced became more and more deformed as it struggled to get to the end of the cylinder or *rouleau*. So the older expression became reinvigorated. It was picked up by the masses and became more informal in register. In the popular imagination, because of the straining sound of the phonograph, it came to be associated with the physical weakness of the very ill and those about to "kick the bucket".

- ***être dans les choux*** – to fail; to lose; to be up the spout*; to be a write-off

Literally: to be in the cabbages

Il faut bien reconnaître qu'ils sont dans les choux et que rien ne pourra les sauver.

You must recognize that they are up the spout and nothing will be able to save them.

The cabbage is a lowly vegetable which was often eaten by the poor when they could afford nothing else. Any expression using the humble cabbage is not likely to be complimentary. This expression dates back to the second half of the 19th century. The origin seems to be that the word *chou* sounds very much like the verb *échouer*, 'to fail'.

- ***être* ou *tomber à l'eau* ou *dans le lac*** – to come to nothing; to fail; to fall through

Literally: to be *or* to fall in the water *or* the lake

Malheureusement, leurs deux premiers projets sont tombés à l'eau.

Unfortunately, their first two projects fell through.

Remember to pronounce the hard c in *lac*!

In fact, **tomber dans le lac** comes from an older expression which has now fallen from use. That expression was **tomber dans le lacs** (where the c and the s were not pronounced). *Le lacs* was 'the snare' so it actually meant 'to fall into the trap'. Little by little the word *lacs* was confused with *le lac*, 'the lake' (where the hard c is pronounced). *Le lac* was then replaced with *l'eau* and the meaning shifted a little to mean 'to fall through'.

- *faire chou blanc* – to draw a blank; to not win anything; to not succeed

Literally: to do white cabbage

Je croyais que ce serait une affaire lucrative, mais j'ai fait chou blanc.

I thought it would be a money-maker, but it wasn't a success.

It seems that the origin of this lovely expression sadly has nothing to do with cabbages. Back in the 16th century, the game of skittles was very popular and *faire coup blanc* meant 'to fail to knock down anything'. In the *berrichon* dialect of the West of France, *coup* was pronounced *chou* and this seems the likeliest explanation of its origin.

- ***les carottes sont cuites*** * – it's all over; your (his, her, etc.) goose is cooked*

Literally: the carrots are cooked

Ils ne vont pas tenir le coup. Les carottes sont cuites.

They are not going to survive. It's all over.

The carrot is another humble vegetable which was a staple food of the poor. In 1694 we find ***ne vivre que de carottes***, 'to live only on carrots', i.e. meanly. Later we have the expression ***avoir ses carottes cuites*** (1878) meaning 'to be dying' (though it is not clear why it had this meaning). Soon after, a slight shift occurred and we reach the expression we have today, ***les carottes sont cuites***, meaning 'it's all over'.

In June 1944 during World War II, ***les carottes sont cuites*** was one of the many coded messages used by *France Libre* on Radio London as a rallying call to the French Resistance to launch Operation Overlord. It was an operation designed to sabotage German communications to slow down their movements.

Notice that *carotte* in French has one r and two t's!

- ***les rats quittent le navire*** – the rats are leaving the sinking ship

Literally: the rats are leaving the ship

Voyant que la situation était sans issue, les rats ont quitté le navire.

Seeing no way out of the situation, the rats left the sinking ship.

Back in the Middle Ages it was hard to forecast an approaching storm. Is it possible that rats were able to sense that a tempest was approaching and, before a ship set sail, the rats ran ashore to avoid sinking with the ship? Maybe. Superstitious sailors certainly believed it. When a business seems to be in trouble, the canny members of staff quickly find employment elsewhere to avoid finding themselves on the dole.

- *rien n'y fait* – it's no good; it's no use

Literally: nothing does on it

Rien n'y faisait. Elle l'avait supplié de ne pas démissionner, mais il y était bien décidé.

It was no use. She had begged him not to hand in his notice, but he was determined to.

Quiz 8

1. *L'accord entre la direction et le syndicat ... Il ne va pas durer.*
a) *bat de l'aile.*
b) *agite ses ailes.*
c) *est sous son aile.*

2. *Je ne comprends rien. Je ... complètement.*
a) *marche*
b) *neige*
c) *nage*

3. *Si nous ne faisons pas ce qui est nécessaire pour sauver l'entreprise, nous allons foncer dans ...*
a) *les mûres.*
b) *le mur.*
c) *la muraille.*

4. *Ma connexion Internet est dans ... et je ne peux pas envoyer de courriels.*
a) *la choucroute*
b) *le chou-fleur*
c) *les choux*

5. *Je sais que c'est difficile mais vous réussirez. Il ne faut pas …*
a) *baisser les mains.*
b) *baisser les bras.*
c) *baiser les bras.*

6. *La catastrophe est inévitable. C'est la fin des …*
a) *carottes.*
b) *choux.*
c) *haricots.*

7. *Quand elle a reçu une lettre de la banque, elle a fondu en larmes. Cela a été … qui a fait déborder le vase.*
a) *la goutte d'eau*
b) *la dernière paille*
c) *la gousse d'ail*

8. *C'est chacun pour soi ! Les … quittent le navire !*
a) *chats*
b) *rats*
c) *souris*

9. *Étant dans l'impossibilité de fournir les fonds nécessaires, il a jeté …*
a) *le savon.*
b) *l'éponge.*
c) *le gant de toilette.*

10. *Ils réclament une aide urgente, car ils sont au bout du ...*
a) *rôle.*
b) *rouleau.*
c) *roulé.*

11. *Si nous ne pouvons pas trouver de soutien financier pour notre projet, il va tomber ...*
a) *à l'eau.*
b) *de l'assiette.*
c) *de l'eau.*

12. *Quand j'ai vu le niveau des autres stagiaires, je ne me suis pas sentie à la hauteur. Je n'étais pas du tout tranquille. J'étais dans ...*
a) *mes petites sandales.*
b) *mes petites chaussures.*
c) *mes petits souliers.*

13. *J'ai passé toute la matinée à essayer de réparer cet ordinateur, mais ...*
a) *rien n'y fait.*
b) *personne n'y fait.*
c) *rien n'en fait.*

14. *Tout semblait perdu. Elle pensait que pour elle les carottes étaient ...*
a) *cuits.*
b) *cuites.*
c) *cuit.*

15. *Ils ont laissé les choses aller à ... et l'usine devra fermer.*
a) *vau-l'eau*
b) *veau-l'eau*
c) *vaut-l'eau*

16. *Il n'a pas suivi les conseils pratiques que je lui ai donnés et par conséquent, il risque fort de ... à l'échec.*
a) *marcher*
b) *couler*
c) *courir*

17. *Il ne se débrouille pas bien. Il ...*
a) *perd pied.*
b) *perd la chaussure.*
c) *perd la main.*

18. *Il a beaucoup de problèmes et il ne s'en sort pas. Il pédale dans ...*
a) *la choucroute.*
b) *les choux de Bruxelles.*
c) *les choux-fleurs.*

19. *J'espère qu'il ne se heurte pas à un problème parce qu'il se noie dans ... !*
a) *une tasse de café*
b) *un gobelet de lait*
c) *un verre d'eau*

20. Dans cette enquête sur la fraude fiscale gigantesque, les policiers font ...
a) *chou blanc.*
b) *chouchou.*
c) *chou de Bruxelles.*

Answers 8

1.	a	11.	a
2.	c	12.	c
3.	b	13.	a
4.	c	14.	b
5.	b	15.	a
6.	c	16.	c
7.	a	17.	a
8.	b	18.	a
9.	b	19.	c
10.	b	20.	a

CHAPTER 9

Discipliner et renvoyer – disciplining and sacking

- *envoyer paître quelqu'un** – to send somebody packing*

Literally: to send somebody to graze

La dernière fois que j'ai demandé une augmentation de salaire, le chef m'a envoyé paître.

The last time I asked for a rise, the boss sent me packing.

This is a very ancient expression. It was used by François Villon, the best-known French poet of the late Middle Ages, in 1461. The verb used to be transitive, so *paître les animaux* meant 'to feed the animals'. These days it is only used intransitively, so it only means 'to graze', not 'to feed'. Still, whether you are sending someone away to eat grass or telling them to take the cattle away to graze, you are still rudely dismissing them and sending them away with a flea in their ear.

- ***envoyer promener** ou **balader quelqu'un*** * ; ***envoyer quelqu'un sur les roses**** – to send somebody packing* or about his business *or* off with a flea in his ear

Literally: to send somebody walking; to send somebody onto the roses

- ***envoyer péter** **** quelqu'un (**dans les fleurs** ou **les roses**)* – to send somebody packing *or* about his business *or* off with a flea in his ear *or* to tell somebody to go to hell**

Literally: to send somebody to fart (in the roses *or* the flowers)

Quand mon chef de rayon est venu me réprimander à la fin d'une journée très difficile, j'ai eu envie de l'envoyer promener.

When my supervisor came to tell me off at the end of a very difficult day, I wanted to send him packing.

It is bad enough to be sent off to go for a walk but being told to go and walk on prickly roses is quite nasty. The addition of the roses only seems to date back to the 1960s. If you really want to be ruder, then telling somebody to go and fart in the flowers might be much more effective!

- *mettre quelqu'un à pied ; être mis à pied* – to suspend somebody *or* to lay somebody off; to be suspended *or* to be laid off

Literally: to put somebody on foot; to be put on foot

Quand elle a été mise à pied, le syndicat a porté l'affaire en arbitrage.

When she was laid off, the union brought the matter to arbitration.

Imagine the disgrace of being deprived of your horse if you are a member of the cavalry. Such was the punishment handed down to grenadiers who made grave professional mistakes. They were *mis à pied* (put on foot) for a few days or even several weeks, depending on the seriousness of their misdemeanours, and were made to clean out the stables. A modern-day version might be to take away your company car, though **être mis à pied** is to do with the taking away of your work, not your transport.

It is quite likely that the expression dates even further back, and not to the military, to the time when the ownership of any horse was a sign of relative prosperity. If you had your work taken away and had to sell your horse as a result, you were left *à pied*.

- *mettre quelqu'un au pas* – to bring somebody into line; to make somebody toe the line

Literally: to put somebody to the step

Le député déclara qu'il était temps de mettre au pas les syndicats des ouvriers du pétrole.

The M.P. declared that it was time to bring the oil-workers' unions into line.

Marcher au pas is 'to march' so I imagine a squadron of soldiers all keeping perfect time. It follows that if you make someone walk in step with you, you are bringing them back into line and making them conform.

- *passer un (bon) savon à quelqu'un* – to give somebody a (good) telling off; to strongly reprimand somebody

Literally: to pass somebody a (good) soap

Elle a insulté un de nos meilleurs clients. Je lui ai passé un bon savon.

She insulted one of our best customers. I gave her a good telling off.

When you imagine someone being soaped down, it doesn't sound like a very violent image, does it? All those lovely soap bubbles – it sounds quite a pleasure! However, in the days of the communal laundry, washing clothes involved not only soaping the garments but also hitting them with a big paddle to get out all of the dirt. As the women were chatting and gossiping, complaining and putting the world to rights, they were also getting very aggressive. From the 18th century, the word *savon* came to mean 'a reprimand' but the idea of a beating got lost over the years.

- *remonter les bretelles à quelqu'un** – to give somebody a piece of one's mind

Literally: to pull up somebody's braces

- *se faire remonter les bretelles** – to get a real tongue-lashing* or dressing-down

Literally: to have one's braces lifted

Il joue au chat et à la souris dans l'entrepôt. C'est vachement dangereux ! Il faut lui remonter les bretelles.

He's playing tag in the warehouse. It's really dangerous! You have to give him a piece of your mind.

It is not known who first came up with this expression but Rey says that it is fairly recent, only dating back to around 1985. There are several possible origins. Firstly, if you are fighting and someone grabs you by the braces, you are forced to come to order. Secondly, if you twang someone's braces, you give them a short, sharp shock, similar in feel to a quick reprimand. And thirdly, if a man is looking messy with droopy trousers and someone comes along and hitches up his braces for him, he suddenly looks much smarter. In the same way, a tongue-lashing might quickly improve someone's behaviour. The English have a similar expression but using a different article of clothing: when you get told off, you might well be told to pull up your socks.

- *secouer les puces à quelqu'un** – to tell *or* tick* somebody off; to give somebody a good telling *or* ticking* off

Literally: to shake somebody's fleas

C'est une fille sympa, vraiment. Elle a juste besoin qu'on lui secoue les puces de temps en temps pour qu'elle se mette à travailler.

She's a nice girl, really. She just needs a good telling off from time to time to get her to start work.

In informal language, *secouer quelqu'un* on its own can mean 'to reprimand somebody' and doesn't necessarily mean to physically shake them. **Secouer les puces** only implies a verbal telling off, not a physical punishment, but some harsh tellings-off can be such a shock to the system that if you were unfortunate enough to have fleas, they would indeed jump!

There is a related expression: **Secoue-toi les puces !*** – Snap out of it* *or* get a move on!

Literally: shake your fleas!

- **sonner les cloches à quelqu'un** – to give somebody a telling off

Literally: to ring somebody's bells

Quand il nous a lâchés en plein milieu du travail, je lui ai sonné les cloches.

When he walked out on us right in the middle of the job, I gave him a right telling off.

The head might be thought of as almost bell-shaped. If you hit a bell, it makes a loud sound and if it is multiplied, the sound is even more powerful. If you reprimand somebody severely, it is like a verbal blow to the head or even several blows to the head.

- *tirer les oreilles à quelqu'un* – to tell somebody off

Literally: to pull somebody's ears

Blanche a oublié de fermer la boutique à clé hier soir et j'ai dû lui tirer les oreilles ce matin.

Blanche forgot to lock the shop last night and I had to tell her off this morning.

These days the reprimand is only verbal and doesn't imply a physical assault.

There is a related expression, *se faire tirer l'oreille* or *les oreilles* (literally to have one's ear *or* ears pulled). Back in Roman times, if a witness did not want to appear before the tribunal, it was decreed by law that they should be brought against their will, pulled by the ears if necessary. The French expression *se faire tirer l'oreille* or *les oreilles* has been used since as early as the 16th century to mean 'to do something reluctantly' or 'to need much persuasion to do something'.

Les manières rudes – rough manner

- *comme un éléphant dans un magasin de porcelaine* – like a bull in a china shop

Literally: like an elephant in a china shop

Nous discutions tranquillement. C'est alors qu'elle a déboulé comme un éléphant dans un magasin de porcelaine.

We were having a calm discussion and then she went and hurtled in like a bull in a china shop.

- *il ne fait pas dans la dentelle** – he's not particular about the details; he doesn't go in for subtleties; he's not one to bother with niceties

Literally: he doesn't make things in lace

Le moins que l'on puisse dire, c'est qu'il ne fait pas dans la dentelle. Avec son franc-parler, je le trouve parfois très brusque.

The least you can say about him is that he doesn't go in for subtleties. He speaks his mind, and at times, I find him very curt.

Before mechanization, the process of lace-making was a very delicate operation involving complex and meticulous work with needles, bobbins or crochet hooks. Someone who was rough and lacking in delicacy could never work "*dans la dentelle*", i.e. in the lace-making trade.

- *il n'y va pas avec le dos de la cuillère** – he certainly doesn't go in for half measures*

Literally: he doesn't go about things with the back of the spoon

Les tarifs viennent d'augmenter de 100 %. Ils n'y vont pas avec le dos de la cuillère !

The prices have just gone up by 100%. They certainly don't go in for half measures!

Though this figurative expression is fairly easy to understand, it is a little strange. It's not as if it is normal to eat with the back of your spoon. You'd have to be really stupid to try to eat your soup that way! So what is being implied is that this is not someone ineffective or a little dim; rather, it is someone who knows how to get things done and goes about his business in a brusque manner without messing around.

ⓘ

The word *cuillère* can also be written *cuiller*. The two words have the same pronunciation.

- *mettre les pieds dans le plat** – to put your foot in it*; to speak with excessive candour

Literally: to put the feet in the dish

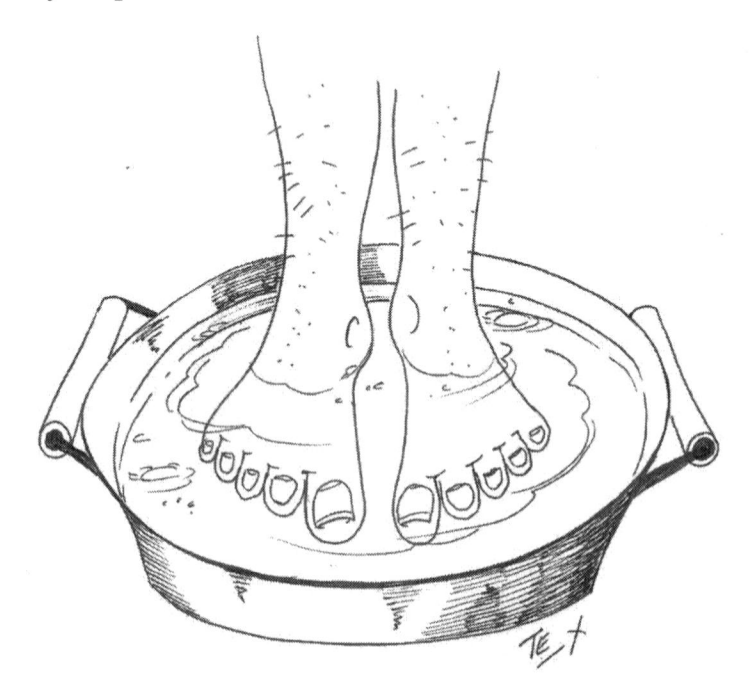

Je voulais aborder une question délicate, mais je n'ai pas voulu mettre les pieds dans le plat.

I wanted to raise a delicate question, but I didn't want to put my foot in it.

You might well imagine that the origin of this expression is perfectly obvious. Someone who stands on the table at a dinner party and puts their foot in a delicious dish would indeed be committing a grave error! However, it seems that the origin lies in a completely different place. It might well be that *le plat* referred to was actually a large expanse of shallow water where you might paddle. The feet would stir up lots of mud, disturbing the clear water. When an indelicate person causes trouble by bringing up a subject others would rather not hear discussed, it is like they are muddying the water by putting their foot in it.

The English expression "to put your foot in it" implies a level of embarrassment on the part of the person making the error. They realize later that they have done something wrong. The French expression is subtly different. Someone may well bring up a subject of discussion which they know others might not want to talk about, but they might feel no embarrassment at having done so, as they pride themselves on their plain speaking.

Faire des affaires ensemble – doing business together

- ***c'est à prendre ou à laisser*** – take it or leave it

Literally: it is to take or to leave

Je ne veux plus en discuter. Voici le prix que je propose. C'est à prendre ou à laisser.

I don't want to discuss it any longer. This is the price I propose. Take it or leave it.

ⓘ

"*A prendre ou à laisser*" (sometimes abbreviated to APOAL and nicknamed "*Les Boîtes*") is the name of a very popular French television game show hosted by Arthur where contestants had to choose boxes to see if they had won a prize. In England the equivalent is the programme "Deal or No Deal". The programme slogan was, "*Le jeu qui rend fou les Français*", 'the game which makes French people crazy'. Do a search on YouTube and you'll probably find a clip of the French version.

- ***c'est dans la poche*** * – it's in the bag*

Literally: it is in the pocket

« *Vous avez conclu le marché avec RVS ?*

– Pas tout à fait, mais je suis sûre que c'est dans la poche. »

"Have you clinched the deal with RVS?"

"Not completely, but I'm sure it's in the bag."

- ***c'est du tout cuit*** * – it'll be or it's a cinch* or a walkover*

Literally: it is ready-cooked

Ne vous inquiétez pas. Ce rachat sera facile. C'est du tout cuit !

Don't worry. This takeover will be simple. It'll be a cinch!

This expression works equally well in the negative: ***c'est pas du tout cuit**** meaning 'it's no easy thing'.

- ***emballez, c'est pesé*** * – it's a deal

Literally: wrap, it is weighed

Et hop ! Tout est réglé. Emballez, c'est pesé.

OK, that's settled then. It's a deal.

This, it seems, was the cry of a famous Parisian market stallholder. He would shout out, "***Emballez, c'est pesé** !*" to tell his co-workers to bag up the goods, as they were ready to go.

(i)

Though this is a business expression, it is also used in other contexts. For example, if a young man has been trying to chat up a woman at a bar and feels he has been successful, he might well turn to his mates and boast, *"Emballez, c'est pesé"*: 'It's a dead cert, I'm in there'.

- *faire affaire avec quelqu'un* – to conclude *or* clinch a deal with somebody

Literally: to make deal with somebody

Je viens de faire affaire avec un client en Angleterre. Quelle est la meilleure façon de se faire payer ?

I've just concluded a deal with a client in England. What is the best way of getting paid?

- *marché conclu* – it's a deal

Literally: market concluded

« *Cent euros.*

– *Quatre-vingts.*

– *Quatre-vingt-dix.*

– *D'accord, marché conclu ! Quatre-vingt-dix euros.* »

"100 €."

"80."

"90."

"O.K. It's a deal! 90 €."

- *passer un marché avec quelqu'un* – to make a deal with somebody

Literally: to pass a market with somebody

Je vais voir le conseil d'administration la semaine prochaine et j'espère pouvoir passer un marché avec eux.

I'm going to see the board of directors next week and I hope to be able to do a deal with them.

Quiz 9

1. *Il ne sert à rien d'avancer comme ... dans un magasin de porcelaine.*
a) *un rhinocéros*
b) *un hippopotame*
c) *un éléphant*

2. *Elle est très indépendante. Je lui ai offert de l'aide, mais elle m'a envoyé ...*
a) *paître.*
b) *pendre.*
c) *partir.*

3. *Voilà, Madame, 400 g de bœuf haché. Emballez, c'est ...*
a) *payé.*
b) *pâté.*
c) *pesé.*

4. *Je suis sûr que nous gagnerons le contrat. C'est du tout ... !*
a) *marché*
b) *cuit*
c) *cuir*

5. J'ai tenté de lui parler, mais il m'a envoyé…
a) *me promener.*
b) *promenade.*
c) *promener.*

6. S'il y a un problème, il vous le dira sans hésitation parce qu'il ne fait pas dans …
a) *le tricot.*
b) *la dentelle.*
c) *le crochet.*

7. Quelle réussite ! J'ai passé … génial avec lui.
a) *une marche*
b) *un marché*
c) *un marchand*

8. Quand elle est arrivée en retard pour la troisième fois cette semaine, je lui ai passé un bon …
a) *savon.*
b) *sentiment.*
c) *saucisson.*

9. Il est très direct et très franc. Vous trouverez qu'il n'y va pas avec le dos …
a) *de la cuillère.*
b) *de la fourchette.*
c) *du couteau.*

10. Elle a cassé une assiette en faisant l'andouille. Je devrai lui sonner ...
a) *la cloche.*
b) *les cloches.*
c) *le clocher.*

11. *Si tu continues à faire l'imbécile, tu vas te faire secouer ... !*
a) *les pouces*
b) *le pouls*
c) *les puces*

12. *Le gouvernement veut mettre ... les grandes entreprises.*
a) *à pas*
b) *au pas*
c) *pas*

13. *Il a été mis .... en raison de son âge ? C'est injuste !*
a) *aux pieds*
b) *à cheval*
c) *à pied*

14. *Hier j'ai oublié d'aller à un rendez-vous important et aujourd'hui, le patron m'a tiré les ...*
a) *oreilles.*
b) *orteils.*
c) *orties.*

15. *Je viens de parler avec M. Rodriguez et il m'assure que le contrat est dans …*
a) *la serviette.*
b) *la poche.*
c) *la valise.*

16. *Le jour où Abel ne s'est pas réveillé à l'heure et est arrivé à l'usine en retard, il s'est sérieusement fait remonter les …*
a) *bretelles.*
b) *bandoulières.*
c) *bandes.*

17. « *On est d'accord ?*
– *Oui, marché …*
a) *conclu !* »
b) *fini !* »
c) *fait !* »

18. *C'est une occasion … prendre ou … laisser.*
a) *à*
b) *de*
c) *en*

19. *Une banque britannique est accusée d'avoir fait … avec des terroristes.*
a) *à faire*
b) *faire*
c) *affaire*

20. Eléna ne veut pas répondre parce qu'elle ne veut pas mettre les pieds dans ..., mais moi je vous dirai la vérité.
a) *le plat*
b) *l'assiette*
c) *les chaussettes*

Answers 9

1. c
2. a
3. c
4. b
5. c
6. b
7. b
8. a
9. a
10. b
11. c
12. b
13. c
14. a
15. b
16. a
17. a
18. a
19. c
20. a

CHAPTER 10

Voir clair et évaluer les problèmes- seeing clearly and evaluating problems

- *arrête ton cinéma !* – Stop making a fuss!

Literally: stop your cinema

J'en ai assez de toutes ces histoires. Arrête ton cinéma !

I'm sick of this to-do. Stop making a fuss!

- *avoir d'autres chats à fouetter* – to have other fish to fry

Literally: to have other cats to whip

Nous perdons notre temps sur cette cause perdue et nous avons d'autres chats à fouetter. Passons maintenant à autre chose.

We are wasting our time on this lost cause and we have other fish to fry. Let's move onto something else.

This expression goes back several hundreds of years but who knows why the poor cat is whipped!

- ***ce n'est pas la mer à boire*** * – it's no big deal

Literally: it is not the sea to drink

Je ne vous ai demandé que de me donner un coup de téléphone de temps en temps. Ce n'est pas la mer à boire !

I only asked you to ring me from time to time. It's no big deal!

This expression is only used in the negative, "*Ce n'est pas la mer à boire*". The idea comes from the fable written by Jean de La Fontaine in the 17th century called "*Les deux Chiens et l'Ane mort*". In this fable, two stupid dogs standing on the shore notice a dead donkey floating on the sea. Being rather hungry, they decide that the best way to get to the animal is to drink all of the water in front of them. That way, eventually, only the donkey will remain. Of course, they die in the process and never get to the food. The moral of the story is that people can be stupid when they become obsessed by an idea. In pursuing their over-ambitious dreams, they get so fired up, that they can't see sense and understand that what they are trying to do is unrealistic. If, on the other hand, somebody has a tendency to give up too soon, you can tell them to keep trying because it is not like trying to drink the sea!

- ***ce n'est pas une grosse affaire*** – it's no big deal; it's nothing to get worked up about

Literally: it is not a big deal

Le chef vient nous voir dans une heure, mais ne vous inquiétez pas, ce n'est pas une grosse affaire !

The boss is coming to see us in an hour, but don't worry, it's nothing to get worked up about!

On the other hand, if someone says to you, "*Ce n'est pas une mince affaire*" (literally it is not a small job), that means, 'it's quite a job' or 'it's no easy task'.

- *ce n'est qu'une tempête dans un verre d'eau* – it's just a storm in a teacup

Literally: it is only a storm in a glass of water

Ne vous inquiétez pas ! Cette affaire fait la une des journaux aujourd'hui, mais on l'aura oubliée demain. Ce n'est qu'une tempête dans un verre d'eau.

Don't worry! This business has hit the headlines today, but by tomorrow it will have been forgotten. It's just a storm in a teacup.

- *c'est l'arbre qui cache la forêt* – you can't see the wood for the trees

Literally: it is the tree which hides the forest

Elle est obsédée par l'importance de cette seule affaire, mais c'est l'arbre qui cache la forêt. Avec ou sans cette affaire, nous allons faire faillite.

She is obsessed by this single deal, but she can't see the wood for the trees. With or without this deal, we are going to go bankrupt.

- ***chercher midi à quatorze heures*** – to complicate things unnecessarily

Literally: to look for midday at 2.00pm

Mais vous cherchez midi à quatorze heures ! C'est tout ce qu'il y a de plus simple. Ne vous créez pas de problèmes !

You are complicating things unnecessarily! It's very straightforward. Don't complicate things!

This isn't the easiest of expressions to get the sense of but it comes down to the stupidity of looking for something in a place it simply can't be.

- *faire le point* – to review things; to take stock

Literally: to take the point *or* the bearing

Avant de dépenser plus d'argent, il faut faire le point sur notre situation financière.

Before spending more money, we need to review our financial situation.

If you are standing on a hilltop in thick fog, the last thing you want to do is go striding off in any old direction, as it's sure to end in disaster. The safest thing to do is to get out a compass and a map and take a bearing. That way you know where you are and where you are going and you are not going to fall over the cliff edge in half a mile. It is a good business strategy to stop and assess your present situation before carefully planning the next move.

- ***il n'est pas né de la dernière pluie*** – he wasn't born yesterday

Literally: he wasn't born from the latest rain

Il a suffisamment d'expérience pour ne pas se laisser faire. Il n'est pas né de la dernière pluie.

He has enough experience not to be manipulated. He wasn't born yesterday.

A shower of rain makes everything seem fresh, and someone born of *la dernière pluie* is going to be a rather recent arrival on the scene. Someone who has been around for a while will have lost their innocence and naiveté and is less likely to be taken in or manipulated by others.

- ***il n'y a pas de quoi en faire une montagne*** – don't make a mountain out of a molehill

Literally: there is nothing to make a mountain about

Ce n'est pas d'une énorme gravité. Il n'y a pas de quoi en faire une montagne.

It's not terribly serious. Don't make a mountain out of a molehill.

(i)

The expression *faire une montagne d'une taupinière* (literally to make a mountain out of a molehill) also exists in French.

- ***monter en épingle*** – to blow something up out of all proportion

Literally: to put up on a pin

Le gouvernement a monté en épingle une petite étude ridicule faite par un universitaire peu connu.

The government has blown out of all proportion a ridiculous small study done by a little-known academic.

It seems this expression refers to jewellery. If a jeweller sets a precious stone upon a pin, he or she is showing it off and is drawing as much attention to it as possible, so if we mount something upon a pin, we are giving it exaggerated importance.

- ***pratiquer la politique de l'autruche*** – to bury one's head in the sand; to ignore voluntarily danger *or* the likelihood of failure

Literally: to practise the policies of the ostrich

On ne peut pas être insouciant et pratiquer la politique de l'autruche. Il faut faire face au danger et agir à l'instant.

You can't be happy-go-lucky and bury your head in the sand. You must face up to the danger and act this instant.

Pliny the Elder, the 1st century Roman thinker, was probably the one to start the legend about the poor ostrich. He wrote that the stupid ostrich will bury its head in the sand when it sees danger approaching because it feels safer if it can't actually see its enemy. It's a nice idea but it is false.

An ostrich digs a large hole for a nest and then the female lays its eggs in it. That way the ostrich and its eggs are slightly camouflaged, as they don't stand out quite so much against the landscape. The ostrich turns its eggs several times a day using its beak and so, when observed from a distance, it looks as though it has its head buried in the sand.

In fact, when an ostrich sees danger approaching, it runs away and tries to get its attacker to follow it away from the nest. It then outruns the aggressor (it can run about 40 miles an hour) and generally its eggs are left safe and sound.

Résoudre des problèmes et surmonter des difficultés – resolving problems and overcoming difficulties

- *passer le cap des difficultés* – to overcome difficulties

Literally: to pass the cape of the difficulties

Notre nouveau gestionnaire des ressources humaines va nous aider à passer le cap de nos difficultés.

Our new human resources manager will help us to overcome our difficulties.

In geography a cape is a piece of land which sticks out into the sea and it can be notoriously difficult to sail around. Cape Horn, for example, is legendary for its dangerous rocks, treacherous currents and massive waves, and getting safely around it can be a titanic struggle.

> ⚡ The p at the end of the word *cap* is pronounced.

- ***payer les pots cassés*** – to pay the price for other people's mistakes

Literally: to pay for the broken pots

La crise économique a frappé notre entreprise et on n'a pas pu hausser les salaires du personnel pendant trois ans. Ce sont encore les ouvriers qui vont payer les pots cassés.

The economic crisis has hit our business and we haven't been able to give pay rises for three years. Once again it will be the workers who pay the price.

- *redresser la barre* – to get things back on an even keel

Literally: to right the helm

Il nous faudra du temps pour redresser la barre et améliorer notre position socio-économique générale.

We will need time to get things back on an even keel and to improve our overall socio-economic situation.

This comes from a sailing term. If you right the helm, you are getting the ship back on course.

Les bosseurs infatigables – tireless workers

- *être la cheville ouvrière* – to be the linchpin *or* the kingpin *or* the mainspring; to be the most important person for the smooth-running of operations

Literally: to be the working pin

L'assistant chef de produit est la véritable cheville ouvrière d'une entreprise.

The assistant product manager is the real linchpin of a company.

You might well have come across the French word *cheville* in the area of anatomy. It means 'ankle'. That really doesn't help us to understand this expression. Delve into a good dictionary and you will find the more technical meaning which is 'a dowel', 'a pin' or 'a peg'. Now we are getting somewhere! *La cheville ouvrière* was an essential mechanical part of an early horse-drawn carriage: it attached the front wheel-axel unit to the main body of the vehicle and no carriage could function without it. It was a pin (*une cheville*) which did lots of work (*œuvrer*: 'to work'). That is how from the early 18th century this figurative expression evolved. If you are ***la cheville ouvrière***, your role is essential for the smooth running of operations.

- ***être toujours sur la brèche*** – to be always beavering away*; to be always on the go; to be in a constant state of alertness *or* readiness

Literally: to be always on the breach

Je crois que tu es incapable d'oublier ton travail pendant une semaine entière. Tu es toujours sur la brèche, même quand tu es en vacances !

I think you are incapable of forgetting your work for a whole week. You are in a constant state of alertness, even when you are on holiday!

According to Alain Rey, *une brèche* in military terms means *'une ouverture dans une enceinte fortifiée'*, 'a breach in a fortification', and this is where he says this metaphor has come from. If you are fighting at the breach, either attacking or defending, you are in the middle of the action.

To some French speakers this expression doesn't mean 'to be always on the go' but rather 'to be in a constant state of readiness or alertness'. The military metaphor still works. If there has been a breach in a fortification, everyone needs to be ready for action, waiting for the next wave of attack.

- **être un bourreau de travail** – to be a workaholic*

Literally: to be an executioner *or* hangman of work

Il passe tout son temps au bureau et néglige sa famille. C'est un bourreau de travail !

He spends all his time at the office and neglects his family. He's a workaholic!

- ***ronger son frein*** – to champ at the bit; to have difficulty containing one's impatience

Literally: to gnaw one's brake

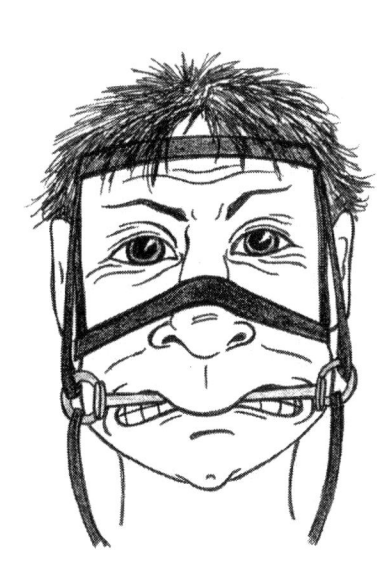

« *Marcel veut commencer dès demain. Il ronge son frein.*

– Oui, il est très impatient ! »

"Marcel wants to start as from tomorrow. He's champing at the bit."

"Yes, he's very impatient!"

You might already know the French word *le frein* meaning 'the brake', as on a car. However, we are not talking about mechanical vehicles here, but rather about horses. In the late 14th century when this expression appeared, *le frein* was another word for *le mors*, the bit which goes between a horse's teeth to help control it. When a horse is keen to get going and is impatiently waiting for its rider, it might well gnaw on its bit in impatience.

There is a related expression, ***prendre le mors aux dents*** – to take the bit between one's teeth *or* to fly off the handle*.

- ***toujours fidèle au poste ? (hum)*** – still manning the fort?

Literally: still *or* always faithful to the post? (humorous)

Beau temps mauvais temps, il est toujours fidèle au poste.

Come rain or shine, you can always rely on him.

This expression probably has its origins in the military. Another useful related expression is ***à vos postes de combat !*** – action stations!

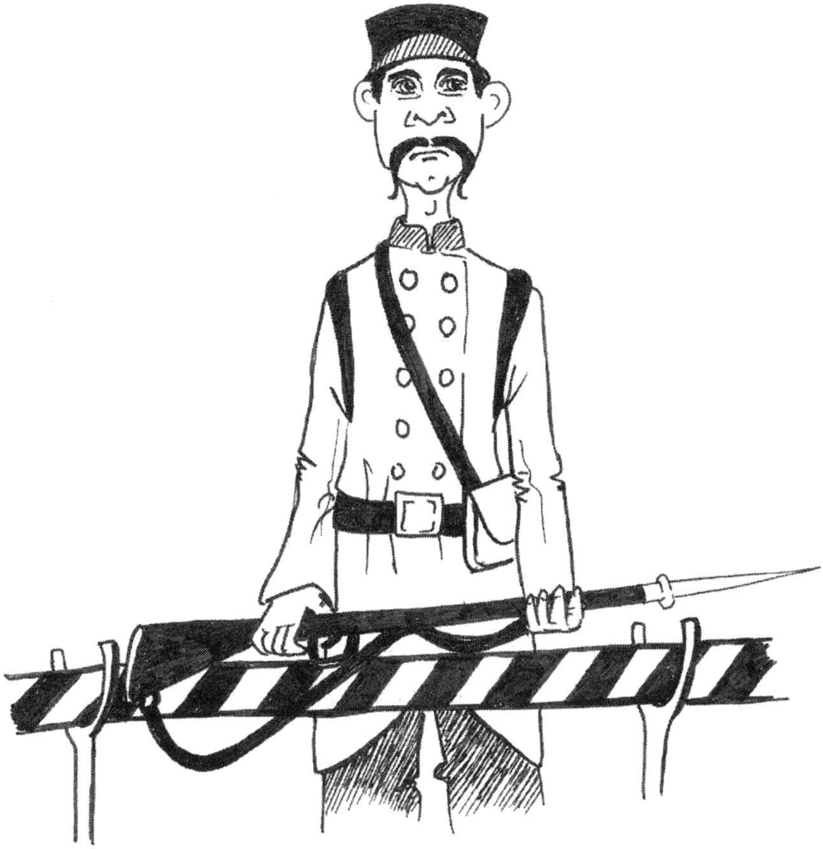

Quiz 10

1. *Notre équipe est toujours sur ... 24 heures sur 24.*
a) *la brèche*
b) *la mèche*
c) *la pêche*

2. *Cette critique n'est pas la fin du monde. Ne la montons pas en ... !*
a) *épingle*
b) *épître*
c) *épinglette*

3. *Son rôle est d'être ... entre l'entreprise et ses clients.*
a) *le cheval ouvrier*
b) *la chèvre ouvrière*
c) *la cheville ouvrière*

4. *Je suis très impatiente. Je ... mon frein.*
a) *ronge*
b) *range*
c) *mange*

5. Ce n'est qu'une tempête dans un verre ...
a) *de vin.*
b) *d'eau.*
c) *de thé.*

6. Avant de nous emballer pour ce nouveau projet, faisons ...
a) *la pointe.*
b) *le pont.*
c) *le point.*

7. Il n'y a pas de quoi en faire...
a) *un montage.*
b) *une montagne.*
c) *une montée.*

8. M. Perrin ne voit pas clair. ...
a) *C'est l'arbre qui cache la forêt.*
b) *C'est l'arbre qui gâche la forêt.*
c) *C'est la forêt qui cache l'arbre.*

9. Je crois que nous avons passé ... des difficultés.
a) *la cape*
b) *le CAPES*
c) *le cap*

10. Ce n'est pas ... à boire !
a) *la mère*
b) *le maire*
c) *la mer*

11. *La patronne du bar a 91 ans et elle est toujours fidèle* ....
a) *à la Poste.*
b) *au poste.*
c) *en poste.*

12. *Pas de problème. Ce n'est pas une grosse ... ! Ça peut attendre.*
a) *affiche*
b) *affaire*
c) *agence*

13. *Il n'a pas de vie sociale parce que c'est ... de travail.*
a) *un baudet*
b) *un bourreau*
c) *un bureau*

14. *Il faut simplement lire ces mots exactement comme ils sont écrits sur la page ...*
a) *Il faut chercher midi à quatorze heures.*
b) *Ne confondez pas midi avec quatorze heures.*
c) *Ne cherchez pas midi à quatorze heures.*

15. *Nous avons fait beaucoup d'erreurs mais maintenant nous allons redresser ...*
a) *le bar.*
b) *la barge.*
c) *la barre.*

16. L'économie est entrée en récession et l'emploi commence à payer …
a) *les pots cassés.*
b) *les meubles cassés.*
c) *la vaisselle cassée.*

17. N'y pensons plus. Nous avons d'autres … à fouetter.
a) *chats*
b) *poissons*
c) *chevaux*

18. Personne ne va l'arnaquer. Elle n'est pas née de la dernière …
a) *averse.*
b) *pluie.*
c) *neige.*

19. N'ayant pas de solutions pour résoudre mes problèmes financiers, je préfère ne pas y penser et pratiquer la politique …
a) *de l'autruche.*
b) *de l'émeu.*
c) *du manchot.*

20. Tu dépasses les limites ! Arrête ton … !
a) *théâtre*
b) *cinéma*
c) *film*

Answers 10

1.	a	11.	b
2.	a	12.	b
3.	c	13.	b
4.	a	14.	c
5.	b	15.	c
6.	c	16.	a
7.	b	17.	a
8.	a	18.	b
9.	c	19.	a
10.	c	20.	b

Afterword

Bravo ! Tu as fini le livre!

Now that you have filled your brain with 200 French expressions, try not to overuse them in your conversations. Use them sparingly or you could end up with this horror:

Il y a quelques années, l'envie m'est venue d'écrire ce livre. **J'ai longtemps rongé mon frein**, *mais je ne voulais pas* **sauter le pas** *parce que j'étais* **un bourreau de travail**, *que j'étais* **toujours sur la brèche**, *prête à basculer dans le* **métro, boulot, dodo**. *J'avais très peu de temps libre, mais* **à cœur vaillant, rien d'impossible !** *Écrire ce livre, ça n'a pas été du gâteau, mais* **je n'ai pas baissé les bras**. **J'ai donné un bon coup de collier** *et j'y suis arrivée à* **la force du poignet** *!*

I have to admit that, after living with this book for so long, I am in danger of falling into this trap myself!

If you have enjoyed this book, please do tell people and leave a review on Amazon. Help to spread the word and hopefully more people will die *moins bête*! If you have any questions or suggestions, please contact me directly at clare@figureoutfrench.com.

À bientôt !
Clare

Complete List of Expressions

CHAPTER 1

Les connaissances – knowledge

apprendre ou *connaître les ficelles du métier** – to learn *or* to know the ropes*

apprendre sur le tas – to learn on the job *or* as one goes along

avoir plus d'une corde à son arc – to have more than one string to one's bow; to have more than one means of reaching one's goal; to be capable of doing several things

connaître ou *savoir sur le bout du doigt* ou *des doigts* – to know off pat* *or* backwards *or* inside out

éclairer la lanterne de quelqu'un – to enlighten somebody

être à même de faire quelque chose – to be able *or* to be in a position to do something

être au courant de quelque chose – to know about something

être dans la course* ; *ne plus être dans la course** – to be in the picture*; to be out of touch

être dans le coup – to be in on it*; to know all about it; to know what's what

je me coucherai moins bête ce soir ; *je mourrai moins bête* – you learn something new every day; you live and learn

savoir, c'est pouvoir (proverbe) – knowledge is power (proverb)

si c'est toujours dans tes cordes – if you are still up to it; if it's still in your line

Être ingénieux et profiter au maximum – being resourceful and making the most of things

faire feu de tout bois – to use any means available

manger à tous les râteliers – to cash in* on all sides; to run with the hare and hunt with the hounds; to take personal benefit from all possible situations without scruples

se débrouiller ou *faire avec les moyens du bord* – to cope as best as one can with what's available; to make do and mend

système D – resourcefulness

tirer le meilleur parti de quelque chose – to make the most *or* the best of something

La diplomatie et la prise de décision – diplomacy and decision making

choisir entre la peste et le choléra – to have to choose one of two bad options; to be between a rock and a hard place; to choose between the devil and the deep blue sea

être assis entre deux chaises ; *avoir le cul entre deux chaises*** ; *être assis le cul entre deux chaises**** – to be caught between two stools; to be in a difficult predicament

ménager la chèvre et le chou – to keep both parties sweet*

CHAPTER 2

Les premiers pas – first steps or going for it

à cœur vaillant, rien d'impossible (proverbe) – nothing is impossible to a willing heart (proverb)

battre le fer tant que ou *pendant qu'il est chaud (proverbe)* – to strike while the iron's hot (proverb)

donner le feu vert à quelqu'un – to give somebody the green light *or* the go-ahead

franchir ou *sauter le pas* – to take the plunge

il n'y a que le premier pas qui coûte (proverbe) – the first step is the hardest

impossible n'est pas français (proverbe) – there's no such word as 'can't'

mettre quelque chose sur pied – to set something up

prendre le taureau par les cornes – to take the bull by the horns

prendre les devants – to make the first move; to take the initiative

se jeter à l'eau – to take the plunge

tenter le coup* – to have a go* *or* a bash at it*; to give it a try *or* a whirl*

vouloir, c'est pouvoir (proverbe) – where there's a will, there's a way (proverb)

Perdre du temps et travailler sans se fatiguer – wasting time and taking it easy at work

avoir une mentalité de fonctionnaire – to have a nine-to-five mentality; to have the mentality of a petty bureaucrat

avoir un poil dans la main* – to be bone-idle*

il est né fatigué – he's bone-idle*

il attend que ça lui tombe tout cuit dans le bec – he's waiting for things to fall into his lap

*on n'est pas là pour enfiler des perles** – let's not waste time

*peigner la girafe** – to waste one's time doing some pointless task or other; to do nothing useful

se la couler douce – to have it easy; to take it easy

se tourner les pouces – to twiddle one's thumbs; to spend time idly doing nothing

CHAPTER 3

Travailler dur – working hard

arriver ou *réussir à la force du poignet* – to manage to do something; to succeed by sheer hard work *or* by the sweat of one's brow

avoir fort à faire (littéraire) – to have one's work cut out

*avoir du pain sur la planche** – to have one's work cut out

c'est en forgeant qu'on devient forgeron (proverbe) – Practice makes perfect (proverb)

*ce n'est pas du gâteau** – it's no picnic*

donner un coup de collier – to put one's back into it; to produce a short and intense burst of effort; to make a big effort

en mettre un coup – to really put one's back into it

être dur à l'ouvrage – to be a tireless worker

faire des pieds et des mains (pour obtenir quelque chose) – to move heaven and earth *or* to bend over backwards (to get something)

gagner son pain à la sueur de son front – to earn a living by the sweat of one's brow

je vais lui montrer de quel bois je me chauffe* – I'll show him what I'm made of; I'm going to show him what I'm capable of; I'm not going down without a fight

ne pas avoir les deux pieds dans le même sabot – to be energetic and dynamic

métro, boulot, dodo – the daily routine of commuting, work then bed; work, work, work!

mettre le paquet – to spare no expense; to pull out all the stops

mettre les bouchées doubles – to work twice as hard; to work quicker; to put on a spurt

se donner un mal de chien pour faire quelque chose – to try really hard *or* to bend over backwards* *or* to bust a gut** to do something

se jeter à corps perdu dans une entreprise ou *la mêlée* – to throw oneself wholeheartedly into a business *or* into the fray

suer sang et eau – to sweat blood (and tears)

un travail de longue haleine – a long job

y mettre du sien – to do one's bit; to make an effort; to be understanding

CHAPTER 4

Les problèmes – Problems

avoir beau faire quelque chose – no matter what one does; whatever one does; to do something in vain

avoir ou *faire deux poids (et) deux mesures* – to have double standards

avoir quelque chose ou *quelqu'un sur les bras** – to have something *or* somebody on one's hands; to be landed with something *or* stuck with something *or* somebody

ça me fait une belle jambe ! (ironique) – a fat lot of good that does me!*

c'est le bouquet !* – that takes the biscuit*; that's just great!(ironic)

c'est trop beau pour être vrai – it's too good to be true

ce serait trop beau ! – that would be too much to hope for!

changer de crémerie* – to take one's business elsewhere; to push off* somewhere else

chercher la petite bête – to split hairs; to nit-pick*; to be extremely meticulous; to do one's best to find mistakes

être dans le pétrin ou *la panade* – to be in a mess* *or* a fix* *or* a jam*; to be in a sticky* *or* embarrassing situation

faire faux bond à quelqu'un – to let somebody down; to leave somebody in the lurch

ficher tout par terre* – to mess everything up

jeter un pavé dans la mare – to set the cat among the pigeons *laisser en plan** – to abandon *or* drop *or* ditch* (a project); to leave in the lurch *or* high and dry (a person)

lever ou *soulever un lièvre* – to hit on a problem; to notice a problem before other people do

mettre des bâtons dans les roues – to put a spanner in the works

se faire pigeonner** ; *se faire prendre* ou *passer pour un pigeon** – to be taken for a ride**; to be had*; to be duped

se plaindre pour un oui (ou) pour un non – to complain over the slightest thing

Identifier ses priorités – prioritizing

de premier plan – key

mettre au premier plan – to consider as the most important issue

mettre au deuxième ou *second plan* – to consider something as of secondary importance

CHAPTER 5

Les professions et les carrières – Professions and careers

avoir les dents longues – to be ambitious; to have one's sights set high

chacun son métier, les vaches seront bien gardées (proverbe) – you should stick to what you know and not meddle with things you don't understand; you do your job and I'll do mine

il n'y a pas de sot métier, il n'y a que de sottes gens (proverbe) – every trade has its value

monter sur les planches – to go on the stage; to tread the boards *vivre de sa plume* – to live by one's pen

Aller bien – going well

ça fait marcher les affaires – it's good for business

c'est une véritable ou *vraie ruche* – It's a hive of activity

construire en dur – to build a permanent structure

être à l'honneur – to have pride of place; to be much in evidence

être au rendez-vous – to be there; to show up

faire boule de neige – to snowball; to catch on quickly; to gather momentum

faire un effet boule de neige – to have a ripple *or* snowball effect

faire des affaires en or – to do a roaring trade

faire le plein – to have a full house; to play to a full house

faire un malheur – to be a big hit; to be all the rage

les petits ruisseaux font les grandes rivières (proverbe) – mighty oaks from little acorns grow (proverb)

marcher du tonnerre (de Dieu) – to be going really well

mettre au point – to perfect (technique); to bring into focus (camera); to develop (invention *or* medicine *or* system); to tune (motor); to finalize (project)

réussir son coup – to carry it off; to pull it off

se vendre comme des petits pains – to sell like hot cakes

un jour à marquer d'une pierre blanche – a very good day which is worth remembering for a long time; a momentous day; a milestone

CHAPTER 6

L'aide et les dettes – help and indebtedness

c'est donnant donnant – it's give and take

donner un coup de main à quelqu'un – to lend somebody a hand

donner un coup de pouce – to give a nudge in the right direction; to help something along

être pistonné* – to have friends who have pulled strings*

obtenir un poste par piston* – to get a job through string-pulling*

se faire pistonner* – to have strings pulled for you*

faire corps – to form one body; to be joined

faire la courte échelle à quelqu'un – to give somebody a leg up *or* a boost; to help somebody overcome an obstacle

j'ai besoin de vos lumières – I need the benefit of your wisdom *or* knowledge

je vous dois une fière chandelle – I am terribly indebted to you

mettre la main à la pâte – to lend a hand; to muck in

prêter main-forte à quelqu'un – to come to somebody's assistance

renvoyer l'ascenseur – to return the favour

se mettre en quatre pour aider quelqu'un ou *pour faire quelque chose* – to bend over backwards to help somebody *or* to do something

se tenir ou *se serrer les coudes* – to stick together

Le travail facile – easy work

c'est le B.A.-BA ou le b.a.-ba (de) – it's the very basics (of); it's the ABC (of)

être au B.A.-BA – to be a beginner

c'est l'enfance de l'art – it's simple

c'est un jeu d'enfant – it's child's play

c'est simple comme bonjour* – it's a cinch**; it's as easy as ABC*; it's as easy as pie*

faire d'une pierre deux coups (proverbe) – to kill two birds with one stone (proverb)

faire quelque chose au pifomètre** ; calculer au pifomètre** – to do something by guesswork; to do a guesstimate*

manger son pain blanc en premier – to have it easy at the start; to start with the best and leave the worst till later

CHAPTER 7

Les heures de travail et les habitudes – Working hours and habits

bosser au black* – to work illegally; to moonlight

faire le pont – to take an extra day off work to make a long week-end of it

faire les trois-huit ; faire les 3 x 8 – to operate round the clock working in eight-hour shifts

prendre le pli de faire quelque chose – to get into the habit of doing something *travailler au noir ; bosser au black** – to work illegally; to moonlight

Avoir de l'influence ou du pouvoir – having influence or power

avoir le bras long – to be influential

être connu comme le loup blanc – to be known all over; to be very well known

être un requin (de la finance) – to be a shark (of the financial world); to be ruthless, greedy and dishonest

être une grosse légume* ou une huile* – to be a bigwig* *or* a big shot*

faire la pluie et le beau temps – to be all powerful; to make all the decisions; to call all the shots

mieux vaut avoir affaire au bon Dieu qu'à ses saints (proverbe) – better to go straight to the top man

Une sale affaire – nasty business

accusé de jouer (un) double jeu – accused of double-dealing

casser du sucre sur le dos de quelqu'un* – to gossip *or* talk about somebody behind his *or* her back

faire des affaires sur le dos de quelqu'un – to do a bit of business at somebody's expense

je ne mange pas de ce pain-là – I'm having nothing to do with that; I'm not stooping to anything like that

la fin justifie les moyens (proverbe) – the end justifies the means (proverb) *les affaires sont les affaires (proverbe)* – business is business (proverb)

prendre des vessies pour des lanternes* – to be fooled *or* badly mistaken

rouler quelqu'un dans la farine* – to pull the wool over somebody's eyes; to deceive *or* dupe somebody

se faire rouler dans la farine* – to be deceived *or* duped; to be had*; to have the wool pulled over one's eyes

tailler un costard* ou *une veste à quelqu'un** – to say nasty things about somebody; to run somebody down behind his *or* her back*; to criticize somebody severely

verser un pot-de-vin à quelqu'un – to bribe somebody

CHAPTER 8

Avoir du mal – struggling

battre de l'aile – to be in a bad way

être dans ses petits souliers – to be like a fish out of water; to feel pretty uncomfortable

je nage complètement* – I'm all at sea*; I'm completely lost

pédaler dans la choucroute** – to be all at sea*; to be struggling and getting nowhere

perdre pied – to be *or* to get out of one's depth; to lose one's footing

se noyer dans un verre d'eau – to make hard weather of the simplest of things

Céder – giving in

baisser les bras – to give in; to throw in the towel

jeter l'éponge – to throw in the towel

la goutte d'eau qui fait déborder le vase – the last straw; the straw that breaks the camel's back

L'*échec* – failure

aller ou *foncer droit dans le mur* –to do something which can only lead to failure; to be heading for disaster

aller ou *s'en aller à vau-l'eau* ou *à la dérive* – to go to the dogs*; to be in a state of collapse; to be on the road to ruin

c'est la fin des haricots* – it's the end of the line; it's a complete disaster; there's no more hope

courir à l'échec – to be heading for failure

être au bout du rouleau – to be exhausted; to have come to the end of the road; to have run out of ideas; to be running short (of money)

être dans les choux– to fail; to lose; to be up the spout*; to be a write-off

être ou *tomber à l'eau* ou *dans le lac** – to come to nothing; to fail; to fall through

faire chou blanc – to draw a blank; to not win anything; to not succeed

les carottes sont cuites* – it's all over, your (his, her, etc.) goose is cooked*

les rats quittent le navire – the rats are leaving the sinking ship

rien n'y fait – it's no good; it's no use

CHAPTER 9

Discipliner et renvoyer – disciplining and sacking

envoyer paître quelqu'un* – to send somebody packing*

envoyer promener ou *balader quelqu'un** ; *envoyer quelqu'un sur les roses** – to send somebody packing* or about his business or off with a flea in his ear

envoyer péter ** quelqu'un (dans les fleurs ou *les roses)* – to send somebody packing or about his business or off with a flea in his ear or to tell somebody to go to hell**

mettre quelqu'un à pied ; *être mis à pied* – to suspend somebody or to lay somebody off; to be suspended or to be laid off

mettre quelqu'un au pas – to bring somebody into line; to make somebody toe the line

passer un (bon) savon à quelqu'un – to give somebody a (good) telling off; to strongly reprimand somebody

remonter les bretelles à quelqu'un* – to give somebody a piece of one's mind

se faire remonter les bretelles* – to get a real tongue-lashing* or dressing-down

secouer les puces à quelqu'un* – to tell or tick* somebody off; to give somebody a good telling or ticking* off

sonner les cloches à quelqu'un – to give somebody a telling off

tirer les oreilles à quelqu'un – to tell somebody off

Les manières rudes – rough manner

comme un éléphant dans un magasin de porcelaine – like a bull in a china shop

il ne fait pas dans la dentelle* – he's not particular about the details; he doesn't go in for subtleties; he's not one to bother with niceties

il n'y va pas avec le dos de la cuillère* – he certainly doesn't go in for half measures*

mettre les pieds dans le plat* – to put your foot in it*; to speak with excessive candour

Faire des affaires ensemble – doing business together

c'est à prendre ou à laisser – take it or leave it

c'est dans la poche* – it's in the bag*

c'est du tout cuit* – it'll be *or* it's a cinch* *or* a walkover*

emballez, c'est pesé* – it's a deal

faire affaire avec quelqu'un – to conclude *or* clinch a deal with somebody

marché conclu – it's a deal

passer un marché avec quelqu'un – to make a deal with somebody

CHAPTER 10

Voir clair et évaluer les problèmes – seeing clearly and getting perspective

arrête ton cinéma ! – Stop making a fuss!

avoir d'autres chats à fouetter – to have other fish to fry *ce n'est pas la mer à boire** – it's no big deal

ce n'est pas une grosse affaire – it's no big deal; it's nothing to get worked up about

ce n'est qu'une tempête dans un verre d'eau – it's just a storm in a teacup

c'est l'arbre qui cache la forêt – you can't see the wood for the trees

chercher midi à quatorze heures – to complicate things unnecessarily

faire le point – to review things; to take stock

il n'est pas né de la dernière pluie – he wasn't born yesterday

il n'y a pas de quoi en faire une montagne – don't make a mountain out of a molehill

monter en épingle – to blow something up out of all proportion

pratiquer la politique de l'autruche – to bury one's head in the sand; to ignore voluntarily danger *or* the likelihood of failure

Résoudre des problèmes et surmonter des difficultés – resolving problems and overcoming difficulties

passer le cap des difficultés – to overcome difficulties

payer les pots cassés – to pay the price for other people's mistakes

redresser la barre – to get things back on an even keel

Les bosseurs infatigables – tireless workers

être la cheville ouvrière – to be the linchpin *or* the kingpin *or* the mainspring; to be the most important person for the smooth-running of operations *être toujours sur la brèche* – to be always beavering away*; to be always on the go; to be in a constant state of alertness *or* readiness

être un bourreau de travail – to be a workaholic*

ronger son frein – to champ at the bit; to have difficulty containing one's impatience

toujours fidèle au poste ? (hum) – still manning the fort?

More about the Author

Clare Jones was born in the North of England in 1960. She fell in love with the French language at the age of 11 and went on to study it to degree level at Leicester University, where she also became a qualified teacher. In 2011 Clare collaborated with Tamsin Edwards to produce an iPhone application, "Figure out French, *Rouler un patin*: to give a French kiss and other French expressions for leisure and health". Though she now lives in England, Clare always has her nose in a French book and she surrounds herself by all things French. She is currently very busy teaching French as a private tutor and when she has the time, she writes a blog on the subject of the French language.

Send her an email at **clare@figureoutfrench.com**

For lessons on Skype, visit her tuition website at **www.frenchtuition-northants.co.uk.**

Like her page on Facebook: **FigureOutFrench**

Follow her on Twitter: **@FigureOutFrench**

Read her blog at **www.figureoutfrench.com**.

More about the Illustrator

Tamsin Edwards studied art at both Nene Art College, Northampton, and Derby School of Art during the early 1980s.

Though well known for her atmospheric watercolour landscapes, Tamsin also creates quirky pen & wash illustrations, often portraying comic images of people and places.

Tamsin has already collaborated with Clare Jones to produce an iPhone application. Past commissioned projects also include the children's storybook 'Tales of Two Shires' and a book of poetic verses.

As well as regularly exhibiting work and selling to clients around the world, Tamsin has also had several paintings published in an international magazine.

To view further examples of her work or to buy original artwork from this book, please visit **www.texart.co.uk/**.

Tamsin can be contacted at **art@texart.co.uk**.

By the same author and illustrator

Mustn't Push Granny in the Nettles: 200 French Expressions

ISBN 9798624943773

Printed by KDP, An Amazon.com Company, 2020

A quirky, illustrated guide to French expressions for learners of French at home, school, evening class or university. Make your French sound more natural and understand more of the figurative language the French use every day, such as **Il ne faut pas pousser mémé dans les orties !** – That's pushing it too far! (Literally: you must not push granny in the nettles!) Chapters include expressions on food and drink, love, laughter, health and happiness.

Learn to speak like the French, preferably without a cat in your throat and a hair on your tongue! Deepen your knowledge by understanding the origins and cultural significance of idioms and test yourself in the multiple-choice quizzes. Then having learned these 200 indispensable French expressions, relax and put your toes in a fan shape, and sleep soundly on your two ears!

Bibliography

BÉARN, Pierre, *Couleurs d'usine*, out of print

BERNET, Charles and RÉZEAU, Pierre, *On va le dire comme ça, Dictionnaire des expressions quotidiennes*, Paris : Balland, 2008

BORTON, Arnold and MAUFFRAIS, Henri, *Learn to Speak Like the French, French Idiomatic Expressions*, Durham: Eloquent Books, 2010

CARADEC, François and POUY Jean-Bernard, *Dictionnaire du français argotique et populaire*, Paris: Larousse, 2009

DUNETON, Claude, *La Puce à l'oreille, Anthologie des expressions populaires avec leur origine*, Le Livre de Poche, 1990

GUIRAUD, Pierre, *Les Locutions françaises*, Presses Universitaires de France, 1973

REY, Alain, *Le Dictionnaire historique de la langue française*, Paris: Dictionnaires Le Robert, 2006

Websites

"**about education**", Laura K Lawless, (collected October, 2015)
http://french.about.com/od/vocabulary/a/mettrelespieds.htm

"**Allocine**" (collected October, 2015)
http://www.allocine.fr/film/fichefilm_gen_cfilm=36129.html

"**American Ostrich Association**" (collected October, 2015)
http://www.ostriches.org/

"**Centre National de Ressources Textuelles et Lexicales**" (collected October, 2015)
http://www.cnrtl.fr/etymologie/pouce

and (collected October, 2015)
http://www.cnrtl.fr/definition/academie8/secouer

"**explic**" (collected October, 2015)
http://www.explic.com/8937-expression.htm

"**Expressio.fr**", Georges Planelles, (collected October, 2015)
http://www.expressio.fr/index.php

"**Figure out French**", Clare Jones's blog (collected October, 2015) http://www.figureoutfrench.com/wp/category/Blog/

You can read more about **expressions with** *tonnerre* in Clare Jones's blog (collected October, 2015) http://www.figureoutfrench.com/wp/2012/07/du-tonnerre-de-dieu/

"*Les deux Chiens et l'Ane mort*" (collected October, 2015) http://www.jdlf.com/lesfables/livreviii/lesdeuxchiensetlanemort

"Les Grands Classiques" (collected October, 2015): "*Le vacher et le garde-chasse*"
http://poesie.webnet.fr/lesgrandsclassiques/poemes/jean_pierre_claris_de_florian/le_vacher_et_le_garde_chasse.html

"Project Gutenberg", *Les Trois Mousquetaires* by Alexandre Dumas (collected October, 2015)
http://www.gutenberg.org/ebooks/13951

"**Se coucher moins bête.fr**" (collected October, 2015) http://secouchermoinsbete.fr/

"Se coucher moins bête" **Facebook** (collected October, 2015) https://www.facebook.com/secouchermoinsbete.fr

"shortédition", Florian's short fable, "*Le singe qui montre la lanterne magique*" (collected October, 2015) http://short-edition.com/classique/jean-pierre-claris-de-florian/le-singe-qui-montre-la-lanterne-magique

" **Le Trésor de la langue française informatisé**", ("le TLFi"), (collected October, 2015) http://atilf.atilf.fr/

Wikipedia (collected October, 2015):

Marie de Vichy-Chamrond
https://en.wikiquote.org/wiki/Marie_Anne_de_Vichy-Chamrond,_marquise_du_Deffand

Saint Denis https://en.wikipedia.org/wiki/Denis

Tino Rossi https://fr.wikipedia.org/wiki/Tino_Rossi

Huppe
https://fr.wikipedia.org/wiki/Huppe_fasci%C3%A9e

Wiktionary (collected October, 2015): **Impossible n'est pas français**
https://fr.wiktionary.org/wiki/impossible_n%E2%80%99est_pas_fran%C3%A7ais and **b.a.-ba**
https://fr.wiktionary.org/wiki/b.a.-ba

INDEX

"8 Femmes" 17

A

affaire avec qn, faire 230

affaires, ça fait marcher les 116

affaire, ce n'est pas une grosse 240

affaire, ce n'est pas une mince 241

affaires en or, faire des 120

affaires sont les affaires, les 171

affaires sur le dos de qn, faire des 168-169

Agincourt, Battle of 37

aile, battre de l'aile 184

arbre qui cache la forêt, c'est l' 241

Arthur 228

ascenseur, renvoyer l' 142

B

B.A.-BA ou *le b.a.-ba (de), le c'est* 145

Bacon, Francis 19

Balzac 53

barre, redresser la 251

bâtons dans les roues, mettre des 99-100

Béarn, Pierre 72

Béart, Emmanuelle 17

beau faire qch, avoir 85

bec, il attend que ça lui tombe tout cuit dans le 49

bête, chercher la petite 92-93

black, bosser au 161

bois je me chauffe, je vais lui montrer de quel 69-70

Bonaparte, Napoléon 41

bond, faire faux 94-95

bouchées doubles, mettre les 73-74

boule de neige, faire 119

bouquet ! c'est le 88

bourreau de travail, être un 254-255

bras, avoir qch ou qn sur les 86-87

bras, baisser les 190

bras long, avoir le 162

brèche, être toujours sur la 253-254

bretelles à qn, remonter les 218-219

C

cap des difficultés, passer le 248-249

carottes sont cuites, les 202

chaises, être assis entre deux 26-28

chandelle, je vous dois une fière 140

Charlemagne 190

Charles VII 37

chats à fouetter, avoir d'autres 238-239

cheville ouvrière, être la 252-253

chèvre et le chou, ménager la 28-29

Chiens et l'Ane mort", "Les deux 240

Chirac, Jacques 175

chou blanc, faire 201

choucroute, pédaler dans la 187-188

choux, être dans les 199

ciel et terre, remuer 68

cinéma !, arrête ton 238

Clavier, Christian 172

cloches à qn, sonner les 220-221

Cœur, Jacques 37

cœur vaillant, rien d'impossible, à 36

corde à son arc, avoir plus d'une 11-12

cordes, si c'est toujours dans tes 20-21

corps, faire 137

corps perdu, se jeter à 75-6

costard ou une veste à qn, tailler un 175

coucherai moins bête ce soir, je me 17-18

coudes, se serrer les 144

coudes, se tenir les 144

couler douce, se la 52

Couleurs d'usine 72

coup de collier, donner un 65-66

coup de main, donner un 133-134

coup de pouce, donner un 134-135

coup, en mettre un 66

coup, être dans le 17

coup, réussir son 124

coup, tenter le 45

courant de qch, être au 15

course, être dans la 16

crémerie, changer de 90-91

cuillère, il n'y va pas avec le dos de la 225-226

cuit, c'est du tout 229

cul entre deux chaises, être assis le 26-28

D

Deffand, Marquise du 40

Deneuve, Catherine 17

Denis, St 40

dentelle, il ne fait pas dans la 223-224

dents longues, avoir les 111-112

dérive, aller ou *s'en aller à la* 195

devants, prendre les 43

dodo !, Fais 73

doigt ou *des doigts, connaître* ou *savoir sur le bout du* 12-13

donnant donnant, c'est 133

Dréville, Jean 172

Dumas, Alexandre 23

Duneton, Claude 63, 168

dur à l'ouvrage, être 66

dur, construire en 118

E

eau, être ou *tomber à l'* 200

eau, se jeter à l', 44

échec, courir à l' 196

échelle, faire la courte 138

Edison 198

éléphant dans un magasin de porcelaine, comme un 222-223

emballez, c'est pesé 229

enfance de l'art, c'est l' 146

envoyer paître qn 212

envoyer péter qn (dans les fleurs ou *les roses)* 213-214

envoyer promener ou *balader qn* 213-214

envoyer qn sur les roses 213-214

épingle, monter en 246

éponge, jeter l' 191

esprit de corps 137

Expressio 10

F

farine, rouler qn dans la 173

farine, se faire rouler dans la 173

fer tant que ou *pendant qu'il est chaud, battre le* 37

feu de tout bois, faire 21-22

feu vert à qn, donner le 38

ficelles du métier, apprendre ou *connaître les* 9-10

fin des haricots, c'est la 195

fin justifie les moyens, la 170-171

flèche de tout bois, faire 21

Florian, Jean-Pierre Clarisse de 14, 113

Fontaine, Jean de La 240

force du poignet, arriver ou *réussir à la* 60-61

forgeron, c'est en forgeant qu'on devient 63-64

fort à faire, avoir 61-62

foutre 96-97

frein, ronger son 255

G

gâteau, ce n'est pas du 64

girafe, peigner la 50-51

goutte d'eau qui fait déborder le vase, la 192

guichets fermés, à 121

H

Haddock, Captain 123

haleine, un travail de longue 78

hiver, habiller qn pour l' 176

honneur, être à l' 118

huile, une 164

Huppert, Isabelle 17

I

impossible n'est pas français 41

J

jambe !, ça me fait une belle 87

jeu, accusé de jouer (un) double 166

jeu d'enfant, c'est un 147

jour à marquer d'une pierre blanche, un 126

jour à marquer d'une pierre noire, un 126

L

Labrune, Jeanne 89

lac, être ou *tomber dans le* 201

lanterne de qn, éclairer la 14-15

Laspalès, Régis 172

légume, être une grosse 164

lièvre, lever ou *soulever un* 98-99

loup blanc, être connu comme le 163

lumières, j'ai besoin de vos 139

M

main à la pâte, mettre la 140-141

main-forte, prêter 141

mal de chien, se donner un 74-75

mal, faire 122

malheur, faire un 121

marché avec qn, passer un 231

marché conclu 230-231

Marois, le général Jean Le 41

même de faire qch, être à 15

mentalité de fonctionnaire, avoir une 45-46

mer à boire, ce n'est pas la 239-240

métier, il n'y a pas de sot 114

métier, les vaches seront bien gardées, chacun son 112-113

métro, boulot, dodo 71-72

midi à quatorze heures, chercher 243

mieux vaut avoir affaire au bon Dieu qu'à ses saints 165

Mirbeau, Octave 172

montagne d'une taupinière, faire une 246

montagne, il n'y a pas de quoi en faire une 246

mors aux dents, prendre le 256

mourrai moins bête, je 17-18

moyens du bord, se débrouiller ou *faire avec les* 24

mur, aller ou *foncer droit dans le* 193

N

nage complètement, je 186

né fatigué, il est 48

noir, travailler au 161-162

O

Operation Overlord 204

oreille or *les oreilles, se faire tirer l'* 221-222

oreilles à qn, tirer les 221-222

oui (ou) pour un non, se plaindre pour un 101-102

ouvrage, être dur à l' 66

Ozon, François 17

P

pain à la sueur de son front, gagner son 68

pain blanc en premier, manger son 150

pain-là, je ne mange pas de ce 169-170

pain sur la planche, avoir du 62-63

pains, se vendre comme des petits 125

panade, être dans la 93-94

"Papa t'es pas dans l'coup" 17

paquet, mettre le 73

parti de qch, tirer le meilleur 25

pas, franchir ou *sauter le* 39

pas, marcher au 216

pas, mettre qn au 216

pas qui coûte, il n'y a que le premier 40-41

patauger 186

pavé dans la mare, jeter un 97

perles, on n'est pas là pour enfiler des 50

peste et le choléra, choisir entre la 26

pétrin, être dans le 93-94

pied, être mis à 214-215

pied, mettre qch sur 42

pied, mettre qn à 214-215

pied, perdre 188

pieds dans le même sabot, ne pas avoir les deux 70-71

pieds dans le plat, mettre les 226

pieds et des mains, faire des 67-68

pierre deux coups, faire d'une 148

pifomètre, calculer au 149

pifomètre, faire qch au 149

pistonné, être 135-136

plan, laisser en 98

plan, mettre au deuxième ou *second* 102-104

plan, mettre au premier 102-104

planches, brûler les 115

planches, monter sur les 114-115

Planelles, Georges 10, 12, 21

plein, faire le 121

pli de faire qch, prendre le 160

Pliny the Elder 248

pluie et le beau temps, faire la 165

pluie, il n'est pas né de la dernière 245

plume, vivre de sa 116

poche, c'est dans la 228-229

poids (et) deux mesures, avoir ou faire deux 85-86

poil dans la main, avoir un 46-47

point, faire le 244

point, mettre au 124

Polignac, cardinal de 40

politique de l'autruche, pratiquer la 247-248

pont, faire le 158

poste ?, toujours fidèle au 256-257

postes de combat !, à vos 256

pot-de-vin à qn, verser un 176

pots cassés, payer les 250

pouces, se tourner les 52-53

poux, chercher des 92

prendre ou à laisser", "A 228

prendre ou à laisser, c'est à 227-228

Project Gutenberg 23

Puce à l'oreille, La 63

puces à qn, secouer les 219-220

puces !, Secoue-toi les 220

Q

quatre pour aider qn, se mettre en 143

R

Raffarin, Jean-Pierre 175

raffarine, la 175

râteliers, manger à tous les 22-23

rats quittent le navire, les 204-205

rendez-vous, être au 118

requin (de la finance), être un 164

Rey, Alain 98, 140, 254

rien n'y fait 205

rouleau, être au bout du 197

ruche, c'est une véritable ou vraie 117

ruisseaux font les grandes rivières, les petits 122

S

sang et eau, suer 77

savoir, c'est pouvoir 19

savoir nager 187

savon à qn, passer un (bon) 216-217

"*Se Coucher Moins Bête*" 19

Sheila 17

simple comme bonjour, c'est 147

singe qui montre la lanterne magique", "*Le* 14-15

souliers, être dans ses petits 185-186

sucre sur le dos de qn, casser du 167-168

"*Sur le bout des doigts*" 13

système D 24

T

tarte, c'est pas de la 64

tas, apprendre sur le 10-11

taureau par les cornes, prendre le 42-43

tempête dans un verre d'eau, ce n'est qu'une 241-242

terre, ficher tout par 95-96

tonnerre (de Dieu), marcher du 123

Trial by Ordeal 190

Trois Mousquetaires, Les 23

trois-huit, faire les 159

trop beau pour être vrai 89

V

vacher et le garde-chasse", "*Le* 113

vau-l'eau, aller ou *s'en aller à* 194

verre d'eau, se noyer dans un 189-190

vessies pour des lanternes, prendre des 172-173

Vichy-Chamrond, Marie Anne de 40

Villon, François 98, 213

Voltaire 40, 86

vouloir, c'est pouvoir 45

W

World War II 204

Y

y mettre du sien 79

Printed in Poland
by Amazon Fulfillment
Poland Sp. z o.o., Wrocław